ITEM 023 273 284

D1078642

Supporting Learners in the Lifelong Learning Sector

Learning Resource Centre
Park Road, Uxbridge Middlesex UB8 1NQ
Renewals: 01895 853326 Enquiries: 01895 853344

Please return this item to the Learning Centre on or before this last date
Stamped below:

1 4 JUN 2010

374. 11

UXBRIDGE COLLEGE
LEARNING CENTRE

Supporting Learners in the Lifelong Learning Sector

Marilyn Fairclough

Open University Press

Open University Press
McGraw-Hill Education
McGraw-Hill House
Shoppenhangers Road
Maidenhead
Berkshire
England
SL6 2QL

email: enquiries@openup.co.uk
world wide web: www.openup.co.uk

and Two Penn Plaza, New York, NY 10121—2289, USA

First published 2008

Copyright © Marilyn Fairclough 2008

All rights reserved. Except for the quotation of short passages for the purpose of
criticism and review, no part of this publication may reproduced, stored in a
retrieval system, or transmitted, in any form or by any means, electronic,
mechanical, photocopying, recording or otherwise, without the prior written
permission of the publisher or a licence from the Copyright Licensing Agency
Limited. Details of such licences (for reprographic reproduction) may be obtained
from the Copyright Licensing Agency Ltd of Saffron House, 6–10 Kirby Street,
London, EC1N 8TS.

A catalogue record of this book is available from the British Library

ISBN-13: 978-0-33-5233625 (pb) 978-0-33-5233632 (hb)
ISBN-10: 0-33-523362-7 (pb) 0-33-523363-5 (hb)

Typeset by Kerrypress, Luton, Bedfordshire
Printed and bound in the UK by Bell and Bain Ltd, Glasgow.

Fictitious names of companies, products, people, characters and/or data that may be
used herein (in case studies or in examples) are not intended to represent any real
individual, company, product or event.

The **McGraw·Hill** Companies

Contents

To Gordon

Preface

This book started out as a booklet I wrote for some students who were working towards a teaching qualification. Usually, when I give my students an assignment, I also suggest an article or book for them to read to supplement what we have covered in class. I could not find anything that dealt specifically with the topic of one assignment: supporting learners. Thus I produced my own text and made copies for the students. The support that learners receive can have such a significant effect on their learning that it deserves a book all of its own – which is what propelled me to develop a slim volume into a complete book.

Marilyn Fairclough

Acknowledgements

Thanks go to:

Fiona Richman at the Open University Press for her advice, guidance, and encouragement.

My family for their support, and in particular my husband Gordon who read each chapter as I wrote it and provided feedback; my son Mike and daughter Katie for giving me new perspectives, and my granddaughter Sophie for her ideas.

Richard White for his advice on all matters relating to the computer and my computer skills. Avril Francome and all the tutors at the Milton Keynes Women and Work Group. Yvonne Elliott and the tutors at Milton Keynes Adult Continuing Education. And all the staff at Haydon Training Business College who have been on my teacher training courses.

Abbreviations

ADHD: Attention Deficit Hyperactivity Disorder

ATLS: Associate Teacher Learning and skills

CPD: Continuing professional development

CTLLS: Certificate in Teaching in the Lifelong Learning Sector

DIUS: Department for Innovation, Universities and Skills

DTLLS: Diploma in Teaching in the Lifelong Learning Sector

GCSE: General Certificate in Secondary Education

ICT: Information and communication technology

IfL: Institute for Learning

LLUK: Lifelong Learning UK

NVQ: National Vocational Qualification

OCN: Open College Network

Ofsted: Office for Students in Education, Children's Services and Skills

OU: Open University

PTLLS: Preparing to teach in the lifelong learning sector

TA: Transactional analysis

U3A: University of the Third Age

QCA: Qualification and Curriculum Authority

QTLS: Qualified Teacher Learning and skills

1 Introduction

Something to think about: Which is more important – the learner or the subject being taught?

What this chapter is about

- Putting the learner at the heart of the learning process
- How this book is set out
- The Qualified Teacher Learning and Skills (QTLS) standards

Putting the learner at the heart of the learning process

I believe that the subject being taught should never take priority over the learners. Neither should the requirements of the qualification. It is for the benefit of the learners and their goals that the subjects and qualifications are offered. Therefore, the focus must be on the learners and how to support them in achieving their goals.

Three conditions are critical in successful learning:

- a learning environment that is friendly and encouraging;
- an open, trusting relationship between the teacher and each learner; and
- a teacher who believes that there is potential in each and every learner

My ideas about teaching were formed very early on in my career. Although I have been teaching in the lifelong learning sector (that is, with learners who are over 16 years old) for the past forty years, I started my teaching in a primary school in Camden Town. Then, Camden Town was a very poor area of London. My pupils were from deprived white families and from Greek Cypriot families. I was given the bottom stream. The bottom stream in this school meant that the pupils found learning extremely difficult and school was not a very joyful experience for them. The way to change that, I realized, was to build warm relationships with the children and to be creative in every lesson, so that whatever the subject, we would all be having fun. The children started to blossom and their feelings of failure were replaced with the pleasures of small successes in their learning.

Since then, I have continued to be drawn to the challenges of winning over reluctant learners and to making unpopular subjects interesting. During one point in my career in further education I was made responsible for General Studies throughout the college. The classes were for students on vocational courses such as motor mechanics, carpentry, engineering, catering, and hairdressing. Traditionally, teachers with unfilled timetables were allocated these unpopular classes. Both teachers and students were bored, and the students often relieved their boredom through disruptive behaviour. I changed the name of the classes from General Studies to Communications and set a variety of tasks such as making videos, giving presentations, planning and organizing trips, and team-building games. This worked well, so I eased out the teachers who did not like teaching these groups and brought in enthusiastic and imaginative part-time teachers.

No subject need be boring. It is a sign of the death knell if a teacher starts off by saying to a class: 'This is going to be a heavy session'. It is our job to think up ways to make a topic interesting and therefore more accessible to learners. This includes classes on induction, health and safety sessions, and theory classes.

Along the way I was often made to re-think what I did. One occasion was at the end of a year when a young apprentice plumber said to me: 'I've really looked forward to your lessons every week but I still don't see the point of Communications'. A compliment, or not? It certainly taught me to start off lessons by explaining the relevance of what we were going to do. Enjoyment is not enough.

This was even more important when I became involved in the introduction of qualifications for teachers who were involved in assessment (the Assessor Awards). Many of the teachers and representatives from industry were openly hostile about both the awards and giving up their precious time. It is off-putting to be faced with several people sitting with arms folded, grumpy expressions, and who are making negative comments. Once they are won over, their resistance to the topic falls away and the whole atmosphere in the class changes.

From these experiences, I learned always to find out in the first few minutes of meeting a new group, who wanted to be in my class and who was there unwillingly.

Schemes for getting young people or the unemployed on the training ladder have had a number of names over the years. I co-ordinated one such scheme for young people. They were regarded as being at the bottom of the heap, and that is pretty much how they regarded themselves. I realized that they first had to be valued by the teachers they came into contact with before there was a chance that they would start to value themselves. Even the huts they were timetabled in gave the message that they were second class.

In my role as an external moderator for Open College Networks, I see many projects involving young people who are homeless, have been in care or prison or excluded from school. I have seen the difference dedicated staff, taking a genuine interest in them, and providing innovative activities that are related to their interests, can make to the young people's attitude to learning. The disinterest is replaced with enthusiasm and there is a new confidence and belief that having achieved one certificate, they can go on to gain more qualifications.

When I was asked to set up a programme for local Asian girls who were leaving school at 16 and who were neither continuing their education nor going out to work, I faced a different set of problems. Their fathers were against the idea because they did not want them to be mixing with boys (or men). I visited the homes with a colleague from their community, got nowhere, and visited again a few months later. Around ten fathers then reluctantly agreed that their daughters could attend a programme, taught by women, but we had to ensure that at break times and lunchtimes the girls never had contact with boys.

This was not too difficult. My mistake was in wanting to spread more widely the good news that such programmes existed. I arranged for a representative from the local paper to come and take photographs. I had not informed myself enough about cultural attitudes. The fathers were scandalized and for a while it looked as though they would withdraw all their daughters.

Assumptions were nearly my downfall when I took the induction session with a group of unemployed adults. It was a new government scheme. There was so little unemployment in my area that the unemployed in this group were long-term unemployed, and did not, I came to think, want to be employed. We met in a classroom, and it was set out in rows of desks – not, when I look back, an environment that adults would be comfortable in, particularly these adults. I was used to getting people to introduce themselves by saying their name and a bit about themselves: whether they were married, how many children they had, what they were interested in. Until then, I had found that people liked to talk about themselves and it was a way of establishing a group rapport. One man took great exception to this. He was very angry. He said he had no intention of talking about his personal life and it was none of my business. He did, however, rather undermine his complaint by saying: 'I don't want everyone knowing that I'm divorced and I live on the Southcourt estate and I go to the hospital for depression.' It had not occurred to me that coming into the school-type setting of a college was humiliating and alien for most of the adults on the programme. Or that I would need to build up trust slowly between them and me and between themselves before they would feel safe speaking openly about themselves.

There are other ways in which people do not feel safe in a learning environment. I like being set tasks where I am thrown in at the deep end, learning by trial and error with a minimum of information. But many people panic and do not know where to start if they are not given clear instructions and guidance.

When the college nurse, who also acted as a counsellor, retired, I set up a college counselling service. I saw first-hand the powerful effect of being listened to. One young man was told to come and see me or he would be expelled. He had kicked in a door and damaged it. I was uncomfortable about being put in this situation, as people should seek counselling voluntarily, not as a threat. I simply asked him: 'What has been going on in your life?' He was feeling misunderstood and unfairly treated because he had been told to appear in court for not having a driving licence, which was still with the driving licence authority. There was no point, he said, going to court, as they would not believe him. We never mentioned the damaged door. Two days later he came bounding up the stairs and told me he had gone to court and the problem was sorted.

In a teaching role, it can be difficult to give individual learners the time to talk. It takes skill to listen to the feelings behind the words, but anxiety, anger, sadness or a lack of confidence can act as a barrier to learning. Sometimes, five or ten minutes of listening and responding in a way that shows the learner you have 'heard' is enough. This can be done without taking time from the main group, or it carrying on for so long that the caretakers are rattling their keys to lock up! Learners come up with unexpected confidences. One trainee teacher hung back after a class and asked me: 'When I am in front of a class, do they see me or do they see a black man?'

I am surprised at the number of partners who feel threatened when their other half joins a class to gain qualifications. New knowledge, understanding, and skills do indeed change a person, and relationships may need to adapt. Sometimes they even fall apart. One learner's husband had mental health problems and hid her coursework. Another middle-aged woman had to get up at five in the morning to do her assignments as her sister was so jealous. It may help to share such problems with the teacher even if the teacher cannot do much about them.

On one occasion, I was observing an art teacher in a young offenders' prison. As soon as I was inside the classroom I was struck by the tranquillity and the calm contentment of the young men. Each one was absorbed in his chosen piece of creativity. It was as though the outside world was sealed off from the classroom. The teacher gave suggestions only if invited to do so and listened to what the individual learners had to say about their artwork. The learners were being given the experience of making their own choices and receiving feedback that increased their self-esteem.

As is clear from the above, it is not easy to get everything right all of the time. Sometimes it is the environment that is wrong. Sometimes it is teachers' assumptions that get in the way because they have not spent enough time trying to understand where the learner is coming from. And sometimes the nature of the relationship between teacher and learner is not trusting enough to be a supportive one when support is needed.

Are some people born teachers? Yes, definitely. Some people seem to be born with a deep interest in, and empathy with, others, and the energy and imagination to make learning a rewarding and exciting journey. Others can be given the knowledge, understanding, and skills to plan and deliver sessions that are varied and meet individual needs. They may not fire up their learners in quite the same way, but they are effective teachers.

It is an uncomfortable fact that some people are not cut out to be teachers. Everyone can recall the destructive effect of having a teacher who is unable to establish good relationships with their learners, or who cannot put over their subject. One suspects these teachers look forward to their sessions with as much reluctance as do their learners. Unfortunately, they can cause a long-lasting negative attitude to learning.

How this book is set out

Each chapter starts with 'Something to think about'. It is intended to challenge what you may currently think. Or it may provide you with insight into something new. This is followed by 'What this chapter is about', which is intended to give you an overview. The chapters then sets tasks for you to do, applying what you have read yourself. Each chapter ends with 'Reflection', giving you the opportunity to reflect on the 'Something to think about' at the start of the chapter. The content of each chapter is cross-referenced to the QTLS standards, which are explained below. Finally, there are some suggestions for further reading or research on websites.

The QTLS standards

Initial teacher training was reformed in 2007, setting out new professional standards (the QTLS standards) and two types of professional status for tutors, trainers, and teachers in the lifelong learning sector (that is, education and training for those over 16). The two types of professional status are:

- Associate Teacher Learning and Skills (ATLS) status: an associate teacher has fewer responsibilities than someone with a full teaching role. Associate teachers may not have to design their own scheme of work or resources. Or they may only teach a subject at one level. This could apply to someone on a full-time contract as well as someone on a part-time contract.
- Qualified Teacher Learning and Skills (QTLS) status: a QTLS teacher is someone with an extensive range of knowledge, understanding, and application of curriculum development, across a range of qualifications and working across larger cohorts. This could also apply to someone on a part-time contract as well as someone on a full-time contract.

Teachers appointed since September 2007 and delivering government-funded training and qualifications must have ATLS or QTLS status. This is awarded by the Institute for Learning (IfL), the professional body for teachers and trainers in the lifelong learning sector. (To find out how to register with the IfL, see the website address at the end of this chapter.)

Newly appointed teachers are required to take the ATLS or QTLS qualifications. However, all teachers, however long they have been teaching, must now comply with Continuing Professional Development (CPD) regulations. Teachers must provide evidence annually to the IfL that they have developed their skills, knowledge, and understanding. The number of hours of CPD per year varies according to the proportion of hours spent teaching. (See Appendix 1 for a more complete explanation.)

The new initial teaching qualifications are based on the new professional standards, produced by Lifelong Learning UK (LLUK), the sector Skills Council for lifelong learning. Each chapter of this book is cross-referenced to the LLUK standards. You can download these from the LLUK website. The following are the six key areas (called 'domains'):

- Domain A: Professional values and practice
- Domain B: Learning and teaching
- Domain C: Specialist learning and teaching
- Domain D: Planning for learning

- Domain E: Assessment for learning
- Domain F: Access and progression

In Appendix 2, you will find the full standards for the professional values, knowledge, and practice for Domain B: Learning and teaching.

Activity

Think back to a time when you were a learner. This could be at school, taking driving or swimming lessons, or a recent course you have been on.

- What positive or negative effect did the learning environment have on you?
- How much did the teacher's belief in your ability to achieve affect your learning?
- How did the level of support you got from the teacher affect your learning?

Reflection

'Which is more important – the learner or the subject?' Do you agree that the learner should be at the heart of the learning process? Or does it make a difference if the subject taught is at an advanced level?

Professional standards

This chapter relates to:

- Domain A: Professional values and practice
  AS4: Reflection and evaluation of their own practice and their continuing professional development as teachers
- Domain B: Learning and teaching
  BP1.1: Establish a purposeful learning environment where learners feel safe, secure, confident and valued

Further reading and useful websites

Tummons, J. (2007) *Becoming a Professional Tutor in the Lifelong Learning Sector*. Exeter: Learning Matters.

www.ifl.ac.uk
www.lifelonglearninguk.org

2 Who are the learners?

Something to think about: Notice on the door of the classroom: 'Everyone is welcome'

What this chapter is about

- Widening participation
- Diversity, inclusivity, and equality
- Learning contexts
- Support needs

Widening participation

There are groups of people who are not in education, training or employment. Somehow they have missed out, or slipped through the net. Groups such as those who:

- left school without any qualifications;
- have been excluded from school;
- are homeless, often young people who have been in care and who are now of the age when they are the responsibility of the Social Services;
- have come to live in the UK, may have limited English skills, and possibly little schooling;
- are offenders in prison or ex-offenders – a high proportion of those in prison lack basic reading, writing, and numeracy skills;
- single parents without qualifications and who need help with childcare before they can enter training;
- have a disability – a physical disability, mental health problems or a learning disability;
- are in an unskilled job offering no training opportunities.

Diversity

Learners are increasingly drawn from these previously neglected groups. This creates new challenges for the teacher. These learners need much support to get the most from their learning. Courses are sometimes set up for learners from the same group, such as offender education. More likely, courses consist of learners who are different from one another in many ways. Think how it must be for the only woman in a group of men, for the only person who prays five times a day, for the person who finds it difficult to make friends. Because they are obviously different from the rest of the group, they can be left out, made to feel not part of the group. Diversity is about:

- valuing difference and
- respecting individuals.

'Everyone is welcome' sums up the message that everyone should be getting.

Creating an environment where diversity is celebrated and valued starts with the teacher. Where a teacher is used to high achievement results, there could be mixed feelings about widening participation. This relates back to whether the subject or the learner is more important. Certainly, there is deep satisfaction from seeing the progress of a learner who has started from a low base. It can seem almost like a miracle.

It can be hard work meeting the needs of a diverse group, especially when those needs make extra demands on the teacher. It needs a lot of patience at times, and an understanding of why a particular learner is responding the way they are. More difficult sometimes, though, is getting a group to be welcoming to everyone within the group. I had a counselling course where one woman was very frosty towards another learner because she said she was too young and had not had enough life experiences. On a construction course, a young man told me the others kept calling him 'gay'. On a care course, the Asian girls and the white girls kept to their separate groups.

Inclusivity

Inclusivity starts with a recognition of our diversity. When planning programmes and sessions, one size will not fit all. To put it another way, plans need to include how we are going to meet diverse interests, experiences, and needs, so that everyone has the opportunity to learn and to achieve.

One way of doing this is to design a session and then to identify where, during the session, individual learners may need support. If a handout is used, one learner may need enlarged print. Another learner may need an alternative assessment activity (using vegetarian ingredients instead of mince to make a lasagne) to evidence what they know or can do. 'Unwitting thoughtlessness' is a good expression to describe the assumptions that we make that we all share the same knowledge and experience. Being inclusive means double-checking the terms used, the examples given, the images presented. It is so easy to churn out the same old materials without revising them. A training consultant was brought in to a college to change the attitude of the lecturers. He used an analogy he had clearly used many times in industry. He told the lecturers they were the equivalent of workers on the car assembly line, and they should respect their superiors. Everyone burst out laughing. He had not adapted his presentation to his audience.

Being inclusive also means bringing on board the learner who has more knowledge or experience than others in the group. They need to be invited to share what they know with the group or to be given more stretching activities. On counselling courses, if learners have worked with the Samaritans or Relate, I may ask them to prepare short talks because they will have a deeper knowledge than I have and will know the answers to a wide range of questions.

One trainer described going to a care home for adults with learning disabilities. His original brief was to give training on fire safety to the care workers. Someone in the organization realized that the residents were being excluded, so they also were invited to join the session. He was delighted at the enthusiasm of the residents, who kept leaping up and shouting out the answers. It is easy to overlook certain groups like those with learning disabilities.

Equality

Equal opportunities and diversity are not interchangeable. They need to go hand in hand. There is no equality of opportunity if difference is not recognized and valued. While valuing and respecting others is key, we must also ensure we work towards getting rid of the inequalities some groups experience. We might recognize that learners come from diverse ethnic groups but we must also have an understanding of different religions and a knowledge of cultural factors.

The following are often seen as barriers to equality:

- age
- disability
- gender
- race/ethnicity
- religious faith/belief
- sexual orientation

We need to check that no-one is barred from attending a course of their choice because of any of these factors. For example, if a learner uses a wheelchair, are ramps and lifts as well as a disabled toilet available?

One trainer was delivering a series of sessions on fire procedures to a group of Ghurkha wives who were employed as cleaners. They had only limited English. He tried having a translator beside him but found it unsatisfactory. He found a website selling DVDs on fire procedures with subtitles in the language of one's choice. He then amended his session plan to incorporate the DVD.

Where learning takes place

Colleges of further education or sixth form colleges may be the first places that spring to mind. They offer qualifications needed to gain entrance to university and vocational qualifications. Courses tend to start in September, and the courses on offer are decided many months in advance, which can result in little opportunity to provide new courses at short notice.

Going to university is not the only way to get a degree. Studying through the Open University enables learners to work from home (or from prison) or to combine a job and study. Learning will increasingly take place in the home as more options become available such as learning through digital TV, podcasts, and the internet. Neighbourhood learning, in community centres, encourages the participation of people living in deprived communities and those in minority groups.

Adult Learning Centres offer courses that do not necessarily lead to qualifications and often cater for people's interests such as foreign language classes, creative studies, computing or fitness classes. They offer many options: a choice of venues, near to where learners live, often local schools, a choice of day- or night-time, and an option to join a beginner, an intermediate or advanced class. Increasingly they are also reaching out to disadvantaged groups and assessing their needs and then setting up tailor-made programmes for them.

In-house training has the advantage of flexibility: it can take place at a time and in a format that is convenient to the organization. Large organizations offer existing qualifications or have designed their own diplomas, recognized by the Qualifications and Curriculum Authority (QCA), ensuring the content is totally relevant to a specific organization. A disadvantage is that there is not the sharing of very different experiences that occurs in less homogenous groups.

Many organizations provide for specific groups, such as:

- people with learning disabilities;
- women who are not in education, training or employment;
- members of ethnic minorities;
- people with mental health problems;
- 14- to-16 year-olds who have been excluded from school;
- young people who are not in education, training or employment and are usually without any skills or qualifications.

Learning can take place in the home, with a peripatetic teacher visiting individual learners. Or the teacher may be dispensed with altogether. Learning circles, which are formed by a group of people with a common interest, and who come together to share what they know and to practise new skills, may use books, television or the internet as resources, but no teacher. Learning also takes place at museums and art galleries, some of it through lectures, some through workshops, and some through worksheets.

Many holidays on offer, including ones abroad or at sea, combine learning with a trip away from home. Learners can choose from cookery, languages, art history, music, art, and so on. They are short intensive courses, with an emphasis on enjoyment.

The range of support needs

There are many barriers to learning, including a lack of information and guidance, attitudes to learning, and problems outside of the classroom. The range and frequency of support needed has increased as participation has widened to include previously neglected groups. The support that many learners require includes:

- information, guidance, and advice about learning options;
- specific information about a chosen course and what it involves;
- study skills and time-management;
- key skills – communication, numeracy, information communication technology (ICT);
- feedback on how well they are doing and how to improve;
- at the end of a course, information on progression onto further courses or employment options;
- references once they have completed their course.

Learners may also need support with:

- finding accommodation
- transport arrangements
- financial assistance
- relationship problems
- health issues
- behavioural problems
- building up self-esteem and confidence
- interpersonal skills
- needs related to a disability

Subsequent chapters will discuss these support needs in more detail.

Activity

Test your knowledge of religions. Answers to the questions are listed at the end of the chapter. You will find further information about religions in Appendix 15.

1 (a) Niqab: what is it and who wears it?
   (b) Yarmulke: what is it and who wears it?
2 Who makes a pilgrimage to:
   (a) Mecca?
   (b) The Ganges?
3 Who worships:
   (a) Brahman?
   (b) Mohammed?
   (c) Buddha?

4 Which religion celebrates each of the following:
   (a) Beltane?
   (b) Yom Kippur?
   (c) Eid ul Fitr?
   (d) Diwali?
   (e) Holi?

5 What are the following:
   (a) Salat?
   (b) Gurdwara?
   (c) Halal?
   (d) Haram?

6 What is the name of the period of fasting in the following religions:
   (a) Christianity?
   (b) Islam?

Reflection

'Everyone is welcome'. How well do you (or would you) create an environment in which one values and respects the differences in all learners?

Professional standards

This chapter relates to:

- Domain A: Professional values and practice
  AS3: Equality, diversity, and inclusion in relation to learners, the workforce, and the community
- Domain B: Learning and teaching
  BS1: Maintaining an inclusive, equitable, and motivating learning environment
- Domain F: Access and progression
  FS1: Encouraging learners to seek initial and further learning opportunities and to use services within the organization

Further reading and useful websites

Tummons, J. (2007) *Becoming a Professional Tutor in the Lifelong Learning Sector*. Exeter: Learning Matters.

www.bbc.co.uk/religion
www.dius.gov.uk/publications
www.equality/humanrights.com
www.qca.org.uk

Answers to the Activity

1 (a) Niqab – a piece of cloth covering the face that some Muslim women wear
   (b) Yarmulke – a Jewish skullcap
2 (a) Muslims make a pilgrimage to Mecca
   (b) Hindus make a pilgrimage to The Ganges
3 (a) Hindus worship Brahman
   (b) Muslims worship Mohammed
   (c) Buddhists worship Buddha
4 (a) Beltane is the Pagan spring festival celebrating the fertility of the coming year
   (b) Yom Kippur is the Jewish Day of Atonement, which ends the Ten Days of Repentance
   (c) Eid ul Fitr is the Festival at the end of Ramadam
   (d) Diwali is the Festival of Light celebrated by Sikhs and Hindus
   (e) Holi is the spring festival when coloured powder and water is thrown
5 (a) Salat: the 5 Islamic daily prayers
   (b) Gurdwara: the name for a Sikh temple
   (c) Halal: food Muslims are allowed to eat
   (d) Haram: food Muslims are forbidden to eat
6 (a) Lent is the name of the Christian fast before Easter
   (b) Ramadam is the name of the month of fasting of Muslims

3   Who gives support?

Something to think about: 'If I do it for you, you will always be dependent on me. If I give you the skills, you won't need me any more'.

What this chapter is about

- The teacher's roles and responsibilities
- Staying within the boundaries of the role
- Support at different points in the learning process
- Internal and external sources of support
- Issues relating to referrals
- Means of support

The teacher's roles and responsibilities

Teachers have a responsibility to keep up to date with health and safety regulations and to comply with them. This includes knowing what to do in the case of fire or if there is an accident or emergency. It means checking the room for trailing wires, for bags left where others can trip over them, as well as checking learners are wearing any safety equipment necessary.

They should keep up to date with legislation concerning equality and human rights and work towards promoting equality and reducing discrimination. At all times they should maintain a professional relationship with their learners. They should also keep up to date with their subject of expertise and engage in continuing professional development.

The scope of a teacher's roles varies. Some teachers are involved in the interviewing, initial assessment, and enrolling of their learners. They are usually responsible for part of the induction process, if not all of it. Usually teachers design their own schemes of work and session plans, but even if there are ready-made ones, they will be expected to adapt them to the needs of different groups.

Assessment *for* learning is a big part of the teaching role. It is how teachers keep a close check on what the learners are learning and how they are learning. It is on-going throughout sessions. This gives an indication of what support learners need. The support could be in the form of coaching or a tutorial. Assessment *of* learning, leading to a qualification, is usually part of the teacher's role, but it may be in the form of an external examination or be the responsibility of someone else in the team.

Keeping records is time consuming, and sometimes teachers cannot see the need for it. They are not only kept because inspectors, internal and external verifiers, and funding agencies require them to be kept; they are kept for the benefit of the learners.

Keeping a register enables teachers to get an overview of a learner's attendance. If attendance is slipping, they can contact the learner and try and get the learner back on track. (A warning: take care how contact is made and that confidentiality is not breached. I once telephoned the home of a learner and spoke to his wife. I said the learner had missed three weeks at college and wondered if he had been ill. There was a silence the other end and then the wife said: 'I thought he WAS at college'.) If there are problems, whether practical or psychological, a mixture of advice and counselling skills can often solve them.

Several years may pass after a course has finished before a learner contacts a teacher for a reference. This is when it is essential to have kept records of the learner's achievements, with dates, and copies of assessments with the feedback given, and any progress reports.

Staying within the boundaries of the role

Teaching is a caring profession and it is tempting to stray beyond the role of the teacher in the desire to support learners, particularly if their needs are great. It is easy to find oneself over-involved in learners' lives. A 16-year-old learner waited until the end of an afternoon session to tell her teacher that she had been made homeless. The teacher and a colleague drove the learner from agency to agency and finally found one that would organize a bed for her. If every agency had turned her away, what would the teachers have done? It was dark and they could hardly drop her off in the street. Is this an instance where the teacher steps out of role? If so, where is the line drawn?

Once, when teaching a group of adult trainee teachers, I realized that a colleague was hanging around every week until my class finished so she could give a lift home, some 15 miles away, to a student who could not drive. He had an air of helplessness about him that got others taking responsibility for him. To me, if the student wanted to become a teacher, he needed to take responsibility for getting himself to and from college. However, a few months later he got a lift to my house to give me some assignments he was behind on. He then asked me to drive him home. He could not get hold of his wife, he said, and there was no public transport between my village and his. I was caught.

We want learners to be responsible for their lives, for their learning, and for the choices they make. When they first come to us, they often need much support, but we need to help them to move from dependence to independence. For this reason, it is good practice to reflect on how positive our help is. If we are too intrusive or we are too ready to take over learners' problems, it is not in the learners' best interests.

Teachers can experience 'burn-out' if they are available at all times. Teachers need break times, but they can find that learners are constantly coming to them during the lunch hour. One group of learners I had responsibility for were very anxious about their ability to write assignments and I made the mistake of giving them my home telephone number, and urging them to contact me if they were stuck. I soon regretted what I had done. My evenings and weekends were peppered with calls. I had to ask them not to telephone any more. E-mails are a perfect solution. My learners can ask me questions and send me drafts of their assignments and I can read them at a time that is at my convenience.

Trying to give support in an area that is outside one's expertise can make the situation worse. It is important to know one's limitations and to refer learners to a specialist. This might be information about employment or further training opportunities, or counselling services.

Some support may need more time than is available. Some learners need a lot of one-to-one support, which would take the teacher away from the rest of the group. It would be better to have a support worker in the classroom. This works well with some learners with disabilities.

Support at different points in the learning process

Support at different points in the learning process can mean success or failure for learners. If support is not provided, the learner can (1) end up on the wrong course, (2) drop out through not being able to keep up or through losing motivation, or through not being supported when temporary personal circumstances arise, or (3) not knowing how to progress when the course is finished.

Learners usually feel flushed with success at the end of a course and full of enthusiasm to do further learning or to find employment. I have seen learners become dispirited because they cannot find a suitable course to move on to. Several learners in one group were eager to move to the next level of training, but the training provider only offered it every other year. They were disappointed enough to consider abandoning their plans. The teacher, however, was able to give them the names of other providers who were offering the course.

Whatever support is given it should be with the intention of promoting learner responsibility and autonomy. Support is not about 'spoon-feeding' learners or making them dependent, it is about giving them the necessary information, skills, and attitudes to help them make their own decisions.

Pre-enrolment

Learners require information, advice, and guidance on what options there are based on their qualifications, goals, and personal situation (for example, a learner may only be free to attend a course on a Saturday or in the evenings). They will then be in a position to make an informed choice.

Before starting on a programme

It is important to identify any barriers there are to learning. Learners may need information, advice or guidance on any of the following:

- *Transport:* disabled learners or young adults living at some distance.
- *Finance:* information for learners who are unemployed or on low incomes.
- *Childcare:* availability of crèche facilities.
- *Basic skills:* arrangements for additional courses if a learner needs support in English or Maths or ICT to benefit from the chosen programme of learning.
- *Learning support:* resources provided for learners with disabilities, which could include a support worker.

At induction

Coming to a new place, a new group, a new learning programme – any, or all of these, can be daunting for anyone. The induction has a significant effect on the subsequent learning experience.

Sometimes induction is carried out by someone other than the class teacher. Indeed, induction can be a lengthy business, up to a week. It may cover a tour of the place of training, health and safety, the expectations of the training provider, their policies and procedures, and available resources such as the library, gym, catering facilities, and counselling services. However, the class teacher still needs to do some induction on the first day as well.

An overview of the course gives learners an insight into the journey that takes them to the qualification at the end: the topics for each session, the learning activities, the formative and summative assessments, and the ways they can access tutorial support.

Joining a new class is entering unknown territory. Looking around at unfamiliar faces and imagining everyone is more confident, more experienced, and more clever than one's self creates apprehension. Worse still, some groups tend to split into subgroups, and there is little whole-group bonding. Learners need to feel safe before they can risk making mistakes, which is a part of the learning process.

'Icebreakers' are useful for helping learners get to know one another. The most common one is for each person to give their name and some other information about themselves. Learners often complain this type of icebreaker is predictable and boring. Waiting for one's turn to speak can be dreadful. Exchanging personal information in pairs and then introducing each other is another well-used method. Some teachers like game-type icebreakers such as preceding a name with an adjective ('I'm curly Caroline', 'I'm dotty Deidre') or getting everyone in a circle and throwing a ball at someone, at the same time saying their name. Not everyone enjoys this type of activity. Teachers need to consider the age and nature of the group members and find ways of relationship-building between them.

Setting boundaries through agreed ground rules creates a feeling of safety for learners: not only mobile phones switched off, no swearing, and no personal headphones, but rules about respect for others – listening without interrupting, the right to hold opinions different from others, allowing everyone an opportunity to speak. Good relationships are more likely to develop within boundaries such as these.

During the course

Many learners of all ages lack time management and study skills. Through discussion and suggestions, learners can be helped to plan their time between classes, and it is important to review with them, especially in the early days, how effectively their plan is working out in practice.

Learners need regular feedback on how they are doing. The assessment activities that occur throughout the lesson give some feedback to learners about their progress: question and answer, and practical and written and oral tasks that are set. In addition, learners value one-to-one discussions with their teacher on their progress. In a large group there may not be time for this to occur on a regular basis. A solution could be to give learners a self-evaluation of their progress to complete, and the teacher can then identify anyone who is having difficulties, and fit in time before or after the session to discuss them.

Near the end of the course

Endings are often abrupt. It is worth giving thought to how the end of a course is structured. There are several strands that need tying up. First, a reflection on what has been learned: this could be orally, asking small groups to prepare posters of what they have learned, or asking pairs to devise questions on their learning to ask other pairs. Second, a look to the future: what are their next steps? The teacher should have to hand information, leaflets, and prospectuses on further training. Learners also need to be told if they can use the teacher as a referee for a course or a job, and whether they need to ask the teacher's permission first before putting their name forward. Finally, one phase of the learners' lives is ending and a new one just beginning. Transitions can be uncomfortable. Friendships have been formed and it is sad to say 'goodbye'. Many groups want to have a celebration of some kind, or to exchange mobile numbers so they can keep in contact.

After the course has ended

Learners may contact the teacher to ask for advice or information after the course has ended. They may, of course, want a reference. Many training providers offering programmes for disadvantaged groups go much further than this. They may have follow-up days or even have a weekly drop-in session when ex-learners can come in for advice and guidance, particularly if they are seeking employment.

Internal and external sources of support

The teacher is, of course, the person with most contact with the learners and will be the chief source of support. But it is important to make use of all the support available both within the organization and outside of it. Teachers cannot be the sole source of support. They have not got the time, expertise or resources.

As we have seen, support is often given by others even before the teacher meets the learners. Schools, probation officers, careers officers and staff within the organization can provide advice and information on courses. Many providers have designated staff who provide further advice and guidance at the enrolment and interviewing stage, and who may undertake an initial assessment. A lot of information is gathered that is relevant to the learner's success or failure. It is thus vital that the information is passed on to the teacher. The teacher may have to ask for the information or they can find late in to the programme that a learner is dyslexic, has behavioural problems or is hard of hearing.

Social and personal problems frequently interfere with learning. The teacher is not expected to deal with housing, financial, transport or childcare problems but they need to know who to refer the learner to in order to get information and advice. Some teachers avoid any involvement in learners' personal problems. Others get over-involved. It is, however, unsupportive to do nothing. If a teacher is uncomfortable with emotional problems or health problems, then it is important that learners are given the opportunity to talk to someone else. It is useful to have posters or leaflets displayed providing information about where to get help.

Responding to personal problems within the boundaries of the teaching role forms the basis of Chapter 12. The teacher can acknowledge and listen to a personal problem but would be unwise to 'solve' it. It is more appropriate to direct the learner to someone trained in helping with personal problems – either within or outside the organization.

Learning support can be given by the teacher within classroom time but at other times it is more effective to use specialist teachers. They are usually from within the organization. Learning needs are identified during the initial assessment period and a learning plan agreed. Some learners have a support worker alongside them in the classroom: learners with a hearing, sight, mobility or learning disability, or with limited language skills.

Peer support is also important. Learners can help each other in the classroom, and this will also help to build the confidence and self-esteem of the helper. Teaching someone else consolidates one's own learning and closes any gaps in understanding.

Issues relating to referrals

It can take time to build up a bank of referral contacts. Keeping a file of leaflets and telephone numbers and adding to it can come in handy when a learner asks for help.

Keeping up to date with people and organizations used for referrals is a problem. Staff move on or change roles. Organizations even change premises. Even so, it is important to try and keep abreast of who to contact and where. For this reason, if you give a learner a number to telephone, it is essential to check if they were successful in making contact. But be careful, of course, not to pry into the outcome. Once you have referred, you are out of the loop. The exception is if you are part of a team working with the learner. Sometimes the learner will want you to make the call or appointment on their behalf.

Issues of confidentiality arise when the person handling the referral asks for information, either verbally or in writing, about the learner. Information should not be given without the consent of the learner. There are no exceptions.

Means of support

The teacher provides support through:

- giving information
- giving advice
- giving guidance
- using counselling skills (not counselling)
- tutorials
- exchange of emails
- reviews
- written information: leaflets, posters, brochures
- writing references

Activity:

Who gives support to your learners?

(a) in the classroom;
(b) within the training organization; and
(c) outside agencies.

Reflection

How easy is it for you to keep within the boundaries of the teaching role when giving learners support? What situations or which learners push the limits of the boundaries?

Professional standards

This chapter relates to:

- Domain A: Professional values and practice
  AS6: The application of agreed codes of practice and the management of a safe environment
- Domain B: Learning and teaching
  BS4: Collaboration with colleagues to support the needs of learners
- Domain F: Access and progression
  FS1: Encouraging learners to seek initial and further learning opportunities and to use services within the organization
  FS2: Providing support for learners within the boundaries of the teacher role
  FS3: Maintaining professional knowledge in order to provide information on opportunities for progression in own specialist area
  FS4: A multi-agency approach to supporting development and progression opportunities for learners

Further reading

Gravells, A. (2007) *Preparing to Teach in the Lifelong Learning Sector*. Exeter: Learning Matters.

Rogers, J. (2008) *Coaching Skills*, 2nd edn. Maidenhead: McGraw-Hill.

4   What's the point of theory?

Something to think about: Teachers were told that certain children in their classes were extremely clever. They were actually only average. At the end of the year these children excelled in their tests. This is known as the Pygmalion effect, or the self-fulfilling prophecy – learners will meet the expectations we have about their stupidity, cleverness, and good or bad behaviour.

What this chapter is about

- Taking a pragmatic approach to theory
- What is learning?
- Multiple intelligences
- Adults and young adults as learners
- Theories of learning
- Motivation
- Counselling theories

Taking a pragmatic approach to theory

Anyone can have a theory. Some people go further and write an article or a book about their theory. Ordinary people are always being asked for their theories of why children are leaving school unable to read or why discipline has broken down. Several people can hold different theories about the same topic, such as how learning takes place. Theories can provide insight into the teaching/learning process and can give teachers helpful tips. But teachers need to test if the theories work for them, with their learners, and apply the theories that are effective and discard the ones that are not.

Theories can explain why things are going wrong in the classroom. Why is it that the learners have remembered nothing of last week's session? Why are learners playing up? Why are learners voting with their feet? Why are learners cooperative the first two weeks and start challenging in the third week?

Theories help teachers justify their choices. Setting aside time to really listen to an angry learner may be seen by some as being soft. Carl Rogers's theories on the powerful effect of empathy, and the difference it makes to a learner to realize someone else understands what they are feeling, can give a teacher the certainty that trying to understand the learner's perspective is the right approach to take.

Certain theories resonate with a teacher more than others. This may be because of the teacher's personality: one teacher may embrace theories that manipulate behaviour, whereas another is drawn towards theories that emphasize the development of the whole person. When a teacher is faced with a very mixed group, or one with disabilities, they will look to theories that will help them meet diverse needs.

It is best to approach theories pragmatically: to pick and choose what is relevant, and to decide for yourself to what extent you agree with the theory in question and then test it out. At the same time, teachers come up with their own theories, and these should not be dismissed just because they are not in print. Teachers should reflect constantly on their teaching and try out new ways of working.

What is learning?

There are many definitions of learning. Wikipedia, the on-line encyclopaedia, has this definition: 'Learning is the acquisition and development of memories and behaviours including skills, knowledge, understanding, values and wisdom. It is the goal of education and the product of experience'.

Learning can take place without a teacher. Teachers may 'teach' something but no-one 'learns' anything, which is a waste of everyone's time

Learning can occur in the classroom without it being taught. This is sometimes called the 'hidden' curriculum or 'unintended outcomes'. Someone can learn that it is better not to volunteer answers in class because there is the probability of being humiliated for giving a wrong answer. Another person, observing tatty, out-of-date posters on the walls, could learn that the staff had little pride in their environment.

Learning may be at one of two levels: surface learning or deep learning. Some learners want to achieve only to gain good marks or a qualification. Some teachers teach at a surface level, concerned only with coaching learners for their assessments. Deep learning involves making links with existing knowledge, understanding, and the application of the new learning to problem-based situations, reading beyond the narrow confines of the assessment, and reflection.

There is more satisfaction from deep learning than surface learning. It is closely linked to two types of motivation: intrinsic motivation and extrinsic motivation. Intrinsic motivation is when one gets satisfaction from learning for its own sake. This leads to lifelong learning. Extrinsic motivation is when one learns to get a reward of some kind, such as a good grade or a certificate. Learning can seem a chore if there is no inner pleasure, and further learning will probably not take place unless there is an external reason. If a teacher makes learning enjoyable and challenging, learners are more likely to use deep learning strategies and to become enthusiastic and committed.

Multiple intelligences

What is 'intelligence'? What counts as intelligence? Could it be that there is not just one sort of intelligence?

Howard Gardner has been influential in education because of his theories about intelligence. He noted that many learners do not excel in tests although they are bright. These learners may have low self-esteem because they are not clever at maths or English, which education has traditionally associated with intelligence, although they may be 'good' at sports or the arts. This can lead to discipline problems, as feeling a failure is a miserable state to be in.

Gardner says there are multiple intelligences. We are born with all of them, but some of our intelligences are more developed than others. This determines the way we learn best. Because of the diversity of how learners' minds work, the teacher needs to look at what each individual does well, and to give them the opportunity to learn through their most developed intelligences. Gardner identified seven (later eight) kinds of intelligences:

- *Verbal-linguistic intelligence:* sensitivity to the meaning and order of words, both spoken and written.
- *Logical-mathematical intelligence:* an ability in maths and complex logical systems.
- *Musical intelligence:* an ability to understand and create music, or to move to music.
- *Bodily-kinaesthetic intelligence:* an ability to use the body for self-expression or towards a goal, such as dance, mime, acting or sports.
- *Spatial intelligence:* a strong visual memory, with an ability to mentally move objects around, such as is needed to be an artist, an engineer or an architect.
- *Interpersonal intelligence:* having an understanding of the motivation and desires of other people, and an ability to work effectively with others.
- *Intrapersonal intelligence:* an ability to understand one's own emotions and, through understanding oneself, be able to live effectively.

A learner who excels on a creative level, or who manages relationships well, is no less intelligent than someone who excels at maths. They just have a different sort of intelligence. The learner who is good at maths may have a poorly developed interpersonal intelligence.

By recognizing that learners have diverse intelligences, teachers can help individuals to develop skills and understanding, by providing diverse learning activities. For example, history (such as Napoleon) could be learned through role play, making models, writing scripts, researching, drawing up statistics or listening to music connected to battles. Above all, it is important to find out what learners do well, and to give full praise, and not to rank one sort of intelligence above another.

Adults and young adults as learners

The lifelong learning sector covers a wide age range, from 16 years to well beyond retirement age. It is not possible to make a sharp division between adults and young adults, but in general it is useful to remember that young adults:

- have fewer life experiences and therefore need more input from the teacher or other sources – discussion as a teaching method can be superficial or not get off the ground because the learners do not have enough knowledge;
- fluctuate in motivation – they may respond well one session and show no interest at all the next, which can be hugely disappointing and bewildering for the teacher;
- are susceptible to peer pressure and peer acceptance – they are not likely to want to stand out from the group;
- mostly need direction – they can be encouraged to agree action plans and targets but need close monitoring;
- are not as sure of themselves as they may appear – they need encouragement and praise.

Malcolm Knowles's theory of andragogy (adult learning theory as opposed to pedagogy, which is the theory of how children learn) assumes that a person becomes an adult when they become self-directing. Adults certainly do not want to be treated as children, but I find that adult learners vary in their capacity or willingness to be self-directing. An unconfident learner initially may want the direction to come from the teacher. But teachers can go too far in expecting adults to be self-directing. One teacher told a new class that they should decide what they wanted to do in each session. She was there just as a facilitator. The group became very annoyed and frustrated, complaining that it was the teacher's job to plan the contents and structure of the programme. By the third week the class had folded.

According to Knowles, adult learners:

- need to know the relevance of what they are learning – this should be an essential part of the introduction to each session, and for any tasks during the session;
- have a wealth of experiences, which need to be drawn upon during sessions;
- need to be responsible for their own decisions and to be treated as though they are capable of self-direction (even if some encouragement is needed to get them to be so);
- will not learn until they are ready and motivated to learn;
- are motivated to learn when they perceive it will help them in life situations, which could account for the big take-up of courses in fitness, personal development, languages, and so on.

Theories of learning

The main schools of theory focus on different aspects and each one has something that adds to our understanding of learning. The Behaviourists are only concerned with what can be observed – that is, behaviour. Cognitive theories focus on thinking processes. Humanists are concerned for the whole person and for feelings. The Behaviourists stress the importance of reinforcement. A stimulus from the teacher (which might be to ask a question, or to set a task) results in a response from the learner (giving an answer, doing an assignment). If the response is rewarded by praise or success, the learner will want to answer future questions or attempt the next assignment. Reinforcement should follow the learner's response as immediately as possible. This has implications for returning learners' assessed work. Once teachers realize the negative effects of returning learners' work late, they make assessment a priority in their 'to do' list, and keep to whatever time scale they have agreed with learners. If a class meets once a week, then work handed in one week should be handed back the following week. Chapter 13 provides more about reinforcement, applied to behaviour problems, and the theory that one reinforces the behaviour one wants learners to do again and ignores or punishes the behaviour that is undesirable.

Behaviourist theory states that a skill is only learned with frequent practice and in varied contexts. This goes back to the difference between teaching and learning. It is not enough to assume a skill has been learned because the learners were able to demonstrate it in lesson three. By lesson five they may well have forgotten how to do it. Consolidation must be built into the lesson plans.

How do people understand, diagnose, and solve problems? Cognitivists suggest we are not passive learners, but we actively organize and create our own meanings when presented with new knowledge, incorporating it into our existing knowledge. As teachers we need to teach learners how to think for themselves and reflect on new knowledge and apply it to new situations. Teachers can help learners with problem solving by:

- 'Divide and conquer': breaking down into smaller steps.
- 'Trial and error': letting learners try to work out problems for themselves. This means not giving out too much information and not leaping in too soon to give help, but waiting until asked. Some learners, however, hate this method, and feel let down. Others thrive on the challenge.
- Asking learners to brainstorm ideas.
- Allowing for an incubation period. The brain can often solve a problem when one has stopped thinking about it actively.

Kolb's Learning Cycle (Figure 4.1) shows the processes a learner needs to go through for learning to occur. For example, on a First Aid course, a learner will have the experience of putting on a sling, then reflecting on the result (perhaps the 'patient's' arm was hanging down too much), drawing conclusions (the sling was not tightened before pinning), and finally planning for the next time they put on a sling (check the position of the arm before pinning).

Some learners enjoy having the experiences and are impatient with the other stages. They do not improve. (These learners would want to move on to bandaging before perfecting their skills at putting on a sling.) Other learners like mulling over experiences without analysing what went well, what did not and why. They are likely to repeat their mistakes. (These learners might laugh with friends about their attempts to put on a sling without identifying what they had done wrong.) A third group like to theorize but do not take any actions. (These learners would discuss the correct way to put on a sling but not put the theory into practice by having another try.)

The teacher's role is to help learners complete the cycle by building in experience, reflection, concluding and action planning into their sessions.

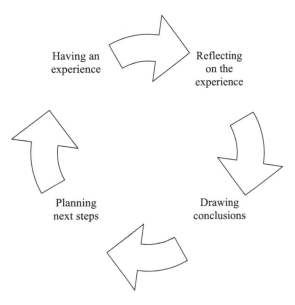

Figure 4.1 Kolb's Learning Cycle

Humanists believe we have an innate drive to learn and develop. At first glance this may seem difficult to agree with. There are too many examples of people who do not want to learn. Carl Rogers, who has had an enormous influence on educational theory, likened human beings to a potato plant he had seen in the cellar of the farm where he was brought up. There was one weedy shoot straining towards the light and warmth outside the cellar window. He concluded that people needed the right conditions to grow and develop themselves, just as with plants. But even if the conditions are poor, both plants and people will still make feeble efforts towards developing their potential to become what they have it in them to become. If we can create an environment conducive to learning, learners will flourish. Humanists also believe that if learners are encouraged to be self-directing and make their own choices, they will be more motivated and thus more successful.

Abraham Maslow, another influential humanist, designed a pyramid (Figure 4.2) to illustrate that the basic needs have to be more or less satisfied before moving onto the next step of the pyramid, and only then can people reach the potential that they are capable of achieving. It is hard for someone to throw themselves into learning if:

- they are very hungry and cold;
- they feel unsafe because of threat from others or homelessness;
- they are not accepted by those around them;
- they lack self-respect and respect from others.

UXBRIDGE COLLEGE
LEARNING CENTRE

Maslow's theory, as with any theory, can be challenged. Some learners, if isolated by others, DO bury themselves in study. However, the most basic needs – for food, water, and air – do, in most cases, have to be met before the next needs on the pyramid become pressing. Young adults, in particular, get very fidgety when it is near lunchtime and tend to be thinking of food rather than the lesson. Older adults start begging for a cup of tea if it is too long since the last cup.

In Chapter 6, we will look at the application of Maslow's theory to the classroom.

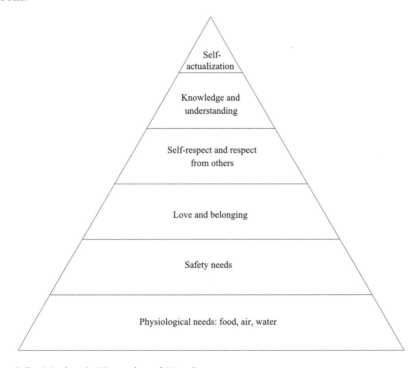

Figure 4.2 Maslow's Hierarchy of Needs

Socrates is sometimes credited with the theory that in order to learn a skill, we move:

- from unconscious incompetence
- to conscious incompetence
- to conscious competence
- to unconscious competence

Before learning to ride a bike, a child would not realize the different skills involved. When they started to learn, they would be aware of how badly they were doing, overbalancing, and not being able to drive in a straight line. Eventually they would be able to ride, but would have to concentrate hard on what they were doing. Finally, they would be able to get on a bike and ride away without having to think what they were doing.

Listening is a skill that many are unaware that they lack, and some think listening is for misguided liberals. They are at the unconscious incompetence stage. These learners need help in realizing that (a) skills in listening will benefit them and (b) they are not currently as good at listening as they think they are. Teachers tend to think learners already have an idea of the skills they lack and the relevance of them. This is not always the case, and learning cannot move from the conscious incompetence stage to the conscious incompetence stage (where they are practising the skills and cannot yet perform the skills without thinking hard about what they are doing) unless learners have been through the first stage. It is therefore essential that teachers stress the relevance to the learner of what they are about to learn. It also helps to reassure learners if they have this model explained to them, as some lose heart when they are at the stage of practising and finding it a struggle.

Motivation

Boredom can kill any motivation to learn. In fact, the need for some excitement can result in the learner creating their own excitement in the classroom, by misbehaving. We need to feel challenged to be roused to learn. But if the challenge is too much, a learner can become anxious to the extent that they perform badly.

Getting the balance right is tricky because learners vary in the amount of challenge they can be placed under. Pitching the level neither too low nor too high, creating an environment where it is seen not only permissible to make mistakes but part of the learning process, and giving frequent feedback and encouragement help to keep learners' stress at a healthy level. Figure 4.3 shows that learners perform better as the level of their arousal or excitement rises, but once they become too anxious, their performance plummets very rapidly. This can happen when learners sit exams or do a driving test.

Teachers can increase motivation if they ensure they:

- build in success so that learners experience the pleasure of doing well;
- explain the purpose and relevance of the session;
- make sessions enjoyable by frequently changing the activity;
- give frequent feedback and praise;
- set achievable targets for each learner.

Counselling theories

Teachers are not counsellors and should not attempt to be. However, counselling theory can give insight into relationships and communication.

Eric Berne's model of the different 'tapes' we use when talking to another person explains why communication is ineffective at times. The three tapes – Parent, Adult, and Child – are somewhat similar to Freud's model of the Id (the raw desires and instincts we are born with), the Superego (which acts as our conscience and which starts to develop around the age of 7), and the Ego (which mediates between

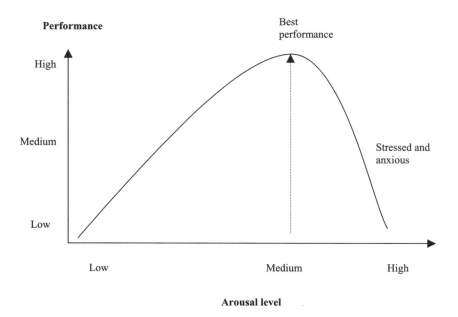

Figure 4.3 Curve of arousal and performance

the Id and the Superego, so some control is exercised but the conscience does not stop all pursuit of desires). The Child tape is natural, creative, and fun loving, but can be manipulative, rebellious or compliant as a result of parental approaches. The Parent tape may be nurturing, or controlling and critical. The Adult tape is rational and logical.

When communicating with others we use different tapes for different situations. By having insight into the tape being used, and the effect it is having, it can help us and others change to a more appropriate tape. For example, I had a large group of electrical engineers for a whole day. One learner regularly got thrown out of classes for his confrontational behaviour. I gave them an activity to do. This was our conversation:

> Learner: Will the marks go towards our final grade? (Adult tape on the surface but with a manipulative Child tape underneath)
>
> Me: No. (Adult tape)
>
> Learner: What will you do if I refuse to do it? (Rebellious Child tape)
>
> Me: I'll burst into tears. (Child tape)
>
> Learner: (laughing) Ok, I'll do it. I don't want you to cry. (Adult tape to my Adult tape)

If I had responded using a critical Parent tape, he would have been delighted and tried to escalate the exchange into a full-blown scene.

It would be a dull teacher who was always in Adult tape mode. Bringing out the fun side of oneself at times is a good thing. Being too nurturing can create dependent learners. While being critical regularly can have a devastating effect on learners, there are cases when it is highly effective to tell a learner that you are very disappointed in them, particularly if you rarely speak in a critical way.

In Chapter 13, we analyse conversations to understand how to turn around undesirable behaviour by using different tapes.

Negative thinking can create a huge barrier to learning. Many learners are burdened with negative thoughts, including:

- I can't do maths
- I'm rubbish at tests
- I'm going to fail
- I can't stand up in front of everyone and speak
- I'll never find the time to do the work

Albert Ellis was a Cognitive-Behaviourist whose method was to challenge the negative thoughts and beliefs that his clients had so that their behaviour was changed (Figures 4.4 and 4.5). An ancient Greek philosopher said; 'It is not events that disturb men, but their interpretation of the events'. Ellis would demonstrate this to his clients with his ABC model:

A: Activating event
B: Interpretation of the event
C: Consequences

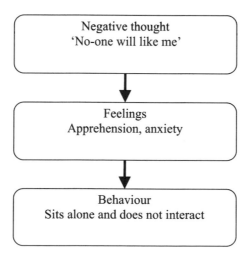

Figure 4.4 Consequences of negative thoughts when joining new group

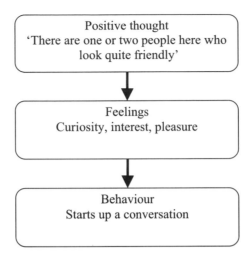

Figure 4.5 Consequences of positive thoughts when joining a new group

If there was a large bang outside in the street, the ABC model for me might be:

    A: Large bang
    B: 'It's a bomb!'
    C: I scream and tremble and hide under the table

Your ABC model might look like this:

    A: Large bang
    B: Sounds like a car backfiring
    C: You carry on working

Ellis would dispute the irrational thoughts and beliefs and get clients to change to more effective thinking.

Teachers can help learners turn negative thoughts into positive ones. For example, if a learner says they have no time to do research and assignments between sessions, the teacher can ask the learner to do a weekly chart of their commitments and leisure activities, and identify an hour when there is a space or there is something the learner is prepared to give up in order to study. Memories of failures from schools days can also be hard to shake off. A good teacher will ensure that the learner is successful in the tasks they are given, and then the teacher has the evidence to challenge the learner when they say they are rubbish. Negative thoughts are deeply ingrained and take time to change. The teacher needs continually to point to the evidence that the learner is achieving.

Carl Rogers stressed the importance of the relationship between a parent and child or teacher and learner to the development of a person. If an infant's parents give unconditional love, that infant will grow up with a sense of self-worth. If, on the other hand, a parent's love is conditional – 'I will withdraw my love when you are not being the person I want you to be' – the infant will grow up burying their essential self and will be conditioned to value themselves according to the values others put on them. This results in a person trying to be what others would like them to be rather than developing the individual potential within them.

When learners have poor self-worth, the teacher's unconditional regard will gradually help the learner to blossom. Unconditional regard means being consistent in valuing the learner as a human being. Thus when a learner's behaviour is undesirable, the behaviour is addressed, but the teacher does not withdraw support or imply that the learner is a worthless being.

Many people have said in later life that one particular teacher has had a life-changing effect on their self-esteem. (And, unfortunately, some poor teachers have had a disastrous effect.)

Activity

Think of a time when you were bored as a learner in a session. Why was this?

1 —
2 —
3 —
4 —
5 —

Recall a session when you were highly motivated as a learner. List the factors that made the session motivating.

1 —
2 —
3 —
4 —
5 —

Reflection

Self-fulfilling prophecy: When you first meet a group, do you mentally sort them into the bright, average, and struggling? Do you think your expectations of what they are capable of influences their eventual achievements?

Professional standards

This chapter relates to:

- Domain A: Professional values and practice
  AS2: Learning, its potential to benefit people emotionally, intellectually, socially and economically, and its contribution to community sustainability

- Domain B: Learning and teaching
  BS3: Communicating effectively and appropriately with learners to enhance learning
- Domain F: Access and progression
  FS2: Providing support for learners within the boundaries of the teacher role

Further reading

Berne, E. (1996) *Games People Play*. New York: Random House.

Curzon, L.B. (2003) *Teaching in Further Education*. London: Continuum International Publishing Group.

Ellis, A. (2005) *How to Stubbornly Refuse to Make Yourself Miserable about Anything – Yes, Anything!*, revised edn. Sacramento, CA: Citadel Press.

Gardner, H. (2006) *Multiple Intelligences – New Horizons in Theory and Practice*, 2nd revised edn. New York: Basic Books.

Knowles, M.S., Holton, E.F. and Swanson, R.A. (2005) *The Adult Learner: The Definitive Classic in Adult Education and Human Resource Development*, 6th edn. Oxford: Butterworth-Heinemann.

Kolb, D.A. (1984) *Experiential Learning: Experience as the Source of Learning and Development*. London: Financial Times/Prentice-Hall.

Lazear, D. (2004) *Higher Order Thinking: The Multiple Intelligences Way*. Brookline, MA: Zephyr Press.

Maslow, A.H. (1998) *Towards a Psychology of Being*, 3rd edn. New York: John Wiley.

Reece, I. and Walker, S. (2003) *Teaching, Training and Learning*, 2nd edn. Houghton-le-Spring, UK: Business Education Publishers Ltd.

Rogers, C.R. (1995) *A Way of Being*. Boston, MA: Houghton Mifflin.

Scales, P. (2008) *Teaching in the Lifelong Learning Sector*. Maidenhead: McGraw-Hill.

Trower, P., Casey, A. and Dryden, W. (1988) *Cognitive-Behavioural Counselling in Action*. London: Sage Publications.

5　What do we need to know about learners?

Something to think about: 'I don't want to know anything about my learners before I meet them. We'll get to know each other and how we are going to do things as we go along'.

What this chapter is about

- Information a teacher needs
- How is the information collected?
- Individual learning plans
- Learner profiles

Information a teacher needs

Before I start teaching a new group, there is a long list of questions I want to have the answers to:

- Why is the learner on the course?
- What are the learner's short- and long-term goals?
- What are their qualifications and experience related to the course?
- Are there any learning difficulties?
- Are there any health problems?
- Are there any personal circumstances that will be barriers to their learning?
- Do they have the functional skills of English, maths, and ICT necessary for the course?
- How do they learn best?
- How will they respond in a group context?
- How can I contact them in between sessions?
- Personal details such a name, address, mobile number, email address, age group, gender, and racial group.

Why do I want to know these things?

First, I need them to plan my scheme of work and session plans and resources. I will have a scheme already, but I may amend it to spend more time on certain topics or leave other topics out. I will include extra resources if I think they will appeal to particular interests or age groups.

I will add more activities requiring learners to use their initiative and imagination in my session plans if most of the group members seem keen to paticipate. If the majority look likely to be passive, I will amend my plans to start off with more teacher-led activities. I will make a note on my plans to draw on the experience I know certain individuals have, and make a note not to assume others already know certain information or have certain experiences.

If I forget to check if the learner has been 'coerced' in some way to join the course, rather than attending because they want to be there, then I deserve any problems I get later. A resentful learner can put a damper on everyone else's pleasure in learning. I find that if I can get any grumbles out in the open right from the beginning, and discuss how they can make the most of a bad job, then there is usually a complete change of attitude and the learner stops resisting learning and joins in with the rest. I also want to gauge the initial level of motivation of individuals and of the group, and if motivation is lukewarm, double the amount of 'selling' I do to arouse interest in the subject.

Learners working for the emergency services may have to miss sessions or suddenly leave a session. They will need to have their mobiles switched on. Parents may need to arrive a bit late or leave a bit early to drop off or collect children from a crèche, childminder or school. It is important to negotiate how these learners will make up for missed sessions or parts of sessions. I usually put the responsibility on them to find out from another member of the group. I have had learners who have left at five in the morning to get to my classes. I am aware that they are tired before they begin and need refreshments to give them a boost before we begin. I also need to ensure I keep them stimulated, so they do not start dozing off.

More people than ever before seem to be in the middle of some domestic crisis or other. A split with a partner, someone in hospital, traumas with house moves, cars off the road, redundancies – they all interfere with concentration. Obviously I do not hear about these sorts of problems during the first session, but by creating an informal atmosphere and keeping my ears and eyes open, I can pick up on them and suggest extensions to assignment dates if it eases the pressure.

I do not want to be thrown into a panic because someone suddenly has an asthma, angina or epileptic attack. If I know ahead that any of these is a possibility and I have discussed what my role is, then I will, I hope, be able to manage the situation calmly. Many people suffer from back problems and get uncomfortable sitting on a hard chair and sitting for a length of time. When there is a change of activity I can ask learners to find a partner from across the room so everyone gets up and changes places. Or I may suggest the learner with the back problem stands up when they feel stiff. What I try to do is minimize anything that prevents the learner from being fully engaged in what we are doing.

Asking for a learner's age or age group has to be justified, otherwise it may fall foul of age discrimination laws. It can be argued that through auditing ages, an organization can show that no-one is excluded from a course because of their age, and it shows the range of ages. Awarding bodies often need the ages of candidates because people may have the same name as someone else, but they are unlikely to have the same birth date.

Occasionally a course is cancelled because of the weather or because the teacher is ill, so it is to save the learners the frustration of turning up needlessly that we need to have a telephone or mobile number. Many teachers now exchange email addresses with their learners so both can make contact in between sessions.

How is the information collected?

Sometimes learners are only required to complete an enrolment form and it is up to the teacher, during the first session, to determine what other information they need. There is a danger here that if the teacher does not recognize the value of this, learner needs are not catered for and the numbers in the class drop off.

At the other end of the scale, learners may go through a lengthy process, such as the following:

- Application form
- CV
- Enrolment form
- Interview
- Assessment of basic skills, paper-based or e-tests
- Learning styles questionnaire
- Individual learning plans
- Induction before the course starts
- Icebreaker on the first day of course

When there are many stages of information gathering, possibly by several different people, that information is not always passed on to the teacher or teachers. It can get stuck in a filing cabinet. I think it is the responsibility of the teacher to chase up the information.

Some teachers say they would rather not know certain information about their learners. For example, they may not want to know that someone has behavioural problems. A learner may have been disruptive at a previous place, but that is not to say they will be so in a different environment. It also can create a self-fulfilling prophecy, with the teacher expecting disruptive behaviour and their expectations then being realized. Certainly, starting a course with a clean slate sounds a nice idea. Personally, I would rather know so I am prepared if it happens. I have found that the rare adult who is difficult is worse than a young adult, and I have been caught on the hop a couple of times.

Early on, when I started training teachers, I was asked to take one of the sessions with psychiatric nurses. I was talking about personality versus character and explaining the Greek meaning of 'persona'. One nurse started shouting out that I did not know what I was talking about. I was taken aback by her rudeness. I invited her to give her own explanation (which was exactly the same as the one I had given). In the coffee break she told a joke that was so obscene I knew she had done it to discomfort me. At the end, one of the other nurses turned to her and said she had ruined the class for her by her attitude. I felt I managed the situation in a feeble way. If I had been warned beforehand, I would have handled the situation better. As it was, I felt out of control.

Individual learning plans

An individual learning plan is a requirement with some courses, but even if it is not, it is a useful document to keep in a simplified form (see Appendix 6). It is a record of an individual's journey from start to finish of the course. It is important that the learner is involved in drawing up the learning plan and understands the purpose of it. The learner identifies their short- and long-term goals, and discusses with the teacher any additional support needs they may have and how they will be met.

If the initial assessment involves taking tests, then these are included, but in other cases all that may be recorded is a simple statement of what a learner has done before. For example, on an ICT course, a learner may be asked if they can send and receive emails and use the internet.

As it is a working document, the learner's progress is charted and, at the end, any achievements noted.

Learner profiles

The following examples show how very useful information can be gathered about individual learners on one form. The imagined course is for an introduction to aromatherapy massage. The results of the learning style questionnaire and the responses to the icebreaker would be filled in by the teacher.

Learner 1

Title: Ms

Surname: Mugabe

First name: Gemma

Age: 25

Nationality: British

Ethnic group: Black African

Health-related problems: None

Reasons for applying for course: I have been a hairdresser for 7 years and I want to add to my qualifications and work freelance

Results of learning style questionnaire: Likes practical hands-on experiences

Response to icebreaker: Warm and confident. Tended to dominate discussions but that may be because no-one else came forward on the first day

Learner 2

Title: Mrs

Surname: Smith

First name: Lily

Age: 38

Nationality: British

Ethnic group: White

Health-related problems: Post-natal depression

Reasons for applying for course: I want to get out of the house one day a week and meet other people and build my confidence through learning something new

Results of the learning style questionnaire: Likes discussions in pairs or small groups

Response to icebreaker: Quiet and unsure of herself. Gemma took her under her wing

Learner 3

Title: Miss

Surname: Ho

First name: Li

Age: 18

Nationality: British

Ethnic group: Chinese

Health-related problems: Registered disabled (uses wheelchair but can move self from wheelchair to another chair)

Reasons for applying for the course: I was in a car accident 18 months ago. I want to be an aromatherapist in a hotel in Thailand

Results of learning style questionnaire: Likes practical activities

Response to icebreaker: Plays down her disability. Quick and imaginative

Learner 4

Title: Mr

Surname: Swift

First name: Martin

Age: 22

Nationality: British

Ethnic group: White

Health-related problems: None

Reasons for applying for the course: I like meeting people and travelling and I want to work on a cruise ship

Results of learning style questionnaire: Likes practical activities

Response to icebreaker: Very outgoing and funny and relaxed in the group. Shared with the group that he is gay

Learner 5

Title: Miss

Surname: Hagger

First name: Dagma

Age: 23

Nationality: Polish

Ethnic group: White

Health-related problems: None

Reasons for applying for the course: I am au pair in England since 6 months. I like a business to set up. Already I have book keeping diploma

Results of learning style questionnaire: Likes theory

Response to icebreaker: Serious. Seems to have difficulty understanding English at times

Armed with this information, a teacher can be better prepared for a new group.

Activity

Read the 5 profiles again and ask yourself:

- The youngest learner is 18 and the oldest 38. Will you need to take this into account?
- How will you take on board the different reasons the learners have for being on the course?
- There is only one male in a group of females. Will there be any issues with the females being massaged by the male?
- How would you build up the confidence of Lily?
- What would you do to ensure the wheelchair user was not disadvantaged when doing the practical tasks?
- Dagmar's comprehension and written English are weak. How would you support her?
- What effect will the personalities of Martin and Gemma have on the classroom atmosphere?

Reflection

Do you think all learners on all courses benefit from discussing their goals and negotiating how they will achieve them? Can this be done during the first session or does it need to be done in one-to-one interviews?

Professional Standards

This chapter relates to:

- Domain A: Professional values and practice
  AS1: All learners, their progress and development, their learning goals and aspirations and the experience they bring to their learning
- Domain D: Planning for learning
  DS2: Learner participation in the planning of their learning

6 Getting the relationships right

Something to think about: Showing genuine interest in learners' lives is important, as is sharing aspects of your own life.

What this chapter is about

- Creating the right environment for learning
- Induction
- Setting the ground rules
- Icebreakers
- Group dynamics
- Teaching styles

Creating the right environment for learning

If the conditions are right, there is a much better chance of learning taking place. The worst scenario would be of a learner sleeping through the alarm, skipping breakfast, arriving late to a new class, where there are two separate groups of people who not only appear to know each other already but are shooting hostile looks at the newcomer, the room is dark and stuffy, and the very first question the teacher asks, the learner gives a wrong answer and there are sniggers from the others. How can a teacher maximize conditions to make learning a pleasant experience?

Returning to Maslow's Hierarchy of Needs, the teacher needs to prepare the room, checking it is at the right temperature, that there is enough light, and that the windows are opened if need be. (Avoid training rooms which are windowless. They are claustrophobic, can cause headaches, it is difficult to control the temperature, and one usually has to have lights on all the time.) Provide water on the tables or advise learners to bring their own, and make sure there are breaks for refreshments. Taking all these steps covers the most basic needs for food, water, and air, which are often referred to as the 'comfort needs' in the context of the classroom.

Making sure learners feel safe is the next task of the teacher. Learners need to learn in an environment where it is safe to make mistakes and in the knowledge that neither the teacher nor peers will make one feel silly. The teacher can do this by establishing a code of conduct and ensuring that all adhere to it. Learners also need to be reassured that they can speak confidentially to the teacher and that what they say will go no further without their agreement. With some subjects this confidentiality will extend to the whole group. If issues such as bereavement, relationships or feelings are being discussed, people tend not to speak openly unless they trust the information will go no further.

What the teacher has little or no control over is if a learner does not feel safe outside the classroom. Maslow's second tier is to do with the safety that comes from having a shelter and all that entails. Some learners become homeless, or have moved out of a care home. Even the psychological effects of selling one home and moving to another can cause plenty of feelings of insecurity. Added to that, home life can be a place where there are tensions, and verbal and physical rows occur – in short, home can be a frightening place. The support the teacher is able to give can range from referring a learner to an agency that can help, and in some cases alerting the appropriate authority to the learner's situation.

The third tier, love and belonging, may sound as if it has no place in the classroom. But learners need to feel they are part of the group and that they have formed friendly relationships with group members. And, very importantly, they need to feel the teacher cares for them as an individual. I have known classes where the teacher does not know the name of everyone in the group. How insignificant must a learner feel when this happens?

Everyone has their own method of learning names. While each learner is introducing themselves to the rest of the group, I make a plan of where they are sitting and I write their name and something that will help me remember them (they look like someone I know, they have their hair in a ponytail, they have freckles, and so on). Then, when I give them a task to do later, I learn their names until I can remember them without looking at my plan. Often I will tell the class at the end of the session that I have been learning their names and I will go round the room saying them. This also helps the group to learn the names, as it is hard to remember them after only hearing them once. Before the next session, I will mentally visualize where everyone sat and go through the names again. I may, of course, come unstuck when the following week the learner with a ponytail has her hair down and people sit in different seats.

Esteem needs are fragile things. We all need to feel we have the respect of others and self-respect. Teachers need to set achievable tasks and give learners the opportunity to demonstrate their strengths. Unfortunately, some people's self-esteem is so low that any amount of praise from the teacher and peers does not convince them that they have earned respect. This can go back to early childhood when love was conditional rather than the child being loved for itself and the learner comes to believe they are worthless, and this has continued. Carl Rogers maintains that a teacher's attitude can turn this around, by consistently treating each individual with care and respect and encouraging the development of the person that is behind the façade they present to the world.

It is only when these needs have more or less been met – the comfort needs, safety needs, love and belonging needs, and esteem needs – that a learner's needs focus on knowledge and understanding. Having this insight, it is easier to work out why some learners do not seem interested, do not participate or are struggling.

Induction

Induction is a golden opportunity to create a good environment for the learners. I use induction to:

- get the group to gel;
- break the ice;
- introduce learners to each other and to me;
- outline the course, the teaching and learning activities, its content and the assessment of the course;
- let learners share their expectations and anxieties about the course;
- agree ground rules.

By asking the learners what they want from the course, I can see if the course is going to match their expectations. Finding out their anxieties gives me the opportunity to explain how the course will unfold. Some of the anxieties on the courses I run are:

- I hope we don't have to do role play
- I'm dreading giving a micro teach
- I'll 'fail' the written assignments
- I won't find the time for the assignments
- There will be too much work involved

I follow these up with activities to do with study skills. Or I explain how each week they learn how to put a session together so that by the time they give their micro teach they are confident and prepared. I encourage them to show me their work early on so that I can make suggestions on their draft.

Setting the ground rules

You can avoid later difficulties by setting the ground rules at the start. It adds to a sense of security if the learners know what is expected. And it prevents misunderstandings and resentment if the rules are clearly set out. Sometimes, I set small groups the task of brainstorming what they expect from me and what they expect from the group. I will then add anything that they have left out. I might print out the ground rules and give everyone a copy. With some groups it is wise to pin the ground rules to the wall. I can then refer to them when someone is breaking a rule. Some rules are negotiable and some are non-negotiable. That will depend on the training organization and the type of group.

With young adults it may be necessary to include such rules as:

- Switch off mobile phones
- Leave headphones in bags
- No swearing
- No fighting

- No eating or drinking
- Listen to others without interrupting
- Show respect to one another
- Remove hats and hoods

It is better if rules are expressed as positives rather than negatives but it is difficult to put 'No swearing' in a positive way. 'Use non-swear words' would sound rather silly.

What should one do if a rule is broken? The sanctions imposed if a rule is broken must be made clear, and they must be enforced. For instance, if someone has their mobile phone on, then it will be taken off them and only returned at the end of the session.

With adults the ground rules might include:

- Respect everyone's opinion
- Support each other
- Participate in activities
- Give everyone a chance to speak

Often there is discussion about participation and sometimes groups want the option to choose not to participate if they are not comfortable about an activity. Personally, I feel if a learner is on a course voluntarily, they need a very good reason to opt out. An example would be that if someone had a bad back, then they might not want to sit on the floor.

Learners often insert a statement about giving everyone a chance to speak because, I think, they have had experience of someone dominating the talking and they do not want a repetition. There is often someone who talks an inappropriate amount of time or who goes off at a tangent. It is important to manage this straight away. I try looking away from the speaker to indicate I am moving onto someone or something else. If the message does not get through, I am blunter and interrupt, saying: 'I want to hear what the others think now'. With one learner who was annoying everyone by his constant comments, the teacher made a joke of it and said she was going to let him talk five times during a lesson and then he could say no more. She had cards with numbers on each card, and would hold up a card each time he spoke until all five had been used up.

What I expect from the learners are along the following lines:

- We will start and end punctually
- Learners phone in if they are unable to attend
- Commitment to the course

Learners can expect the following from me:

- I will assess and return any work given to me the next session
- I will be fully prepared for each session
- I will support learners via email in between sessions

Icebreakers

I introduce an icebreaker as soon as possible because I do not like looking at a group of people facing me in frozen isolation. The quicker I can get everyone talking and relaxing the better. As each learner comes into the room I move towards them and smile broadly and say 'Hello, I'm Marilyn Fairclough', and ask them if they had a long journey and tell them to help themselves to a drink. I introduce them to the person sitting next to them and hope that this will remove a little of the strangeness.

There are different views on which icebreakers to use. Some people groan at being put into pairs and finding out about their partner and then telling the rest of the group. Others are acutely embarrassed at being asked to introduce themselves with an adjective starting off with the same letter of the alphabet as their first name. 'Jolly Jane', 'Boozy Brenda', and 'Enigmatic Edward' is not everyone's cup of tea. These games do, however, do the job of getting to know one another.

An icebreaker that seems to work well and serves more than one purpose is one I saw on the first day of a beginners' German course. The learners were put into groups with large sheets of paper and coloured pens. Once they had told each other their names they had to brainstorm any German names they already knew: cars, rivers, food, drinks, and so on. This not only got them talking naturally to one another, the task they were given boosted their confidence at the realization that they were already familiar with many German words, and also it served as an introduction to the subject.

Another teacher starts every lesson with an icebreaker. Her learners come in and slump in their chairs and appear apathetic. Once she gives them an activity to wake up their motivation and get their brains thinking, they are ready to participate in the lesson proper. More icebreakers are provided in Appendix 3.

Group dynamics

Bruce Tuckman noticed that all groups go through a sequence of stages:

- Forming
- Storming
- Norming
- Performing
- Mourning/ deforming

When a group first gets together they are at the *forming* stage, where first impressions are important and there is a high dependence on the teacher for guidance and direction. Icebreakers and pair or small group work will allow learners to get to know one another. Sharing expectations and previous experiences help to form common bonds. Negotiated ground rules set clear boundaries.

After the first session or two, people start to assert themselves, vying for position as the cleverest, the class clown, the leader. Cliques may form. Some may challenge the teacher. This is the *storming* stage and the teacher has to remember not to take it personally. They can help the group move on to the next stage by encouraging discussions with the whole group and a reminder of the ground rules if necessary. The aim is to clear the air and to stop factions forming.

With good management the storming stage is short-lived and the group starts to gel and to settle down, all moving in the same direction, knowing their own role. This is the *norming* stage, where the teacher can help by moving individuals around so they can develop relationships with everyone in the group. The group is now ready for the *performing* stage, where they can get on with tasks and, as they gain in confidence, have a certain amount of autonomy. The teacher needs to give plenty of feedback and to encourage self-assessment.

At the end of a course there is a sense of achievement but often a sense of insecurity or sadness at moving on and the group splitting up. This is the *mourning* or *deforming* stage. Here, the teacher can discuss options for progression. Groups usually like some sort of celebration to mark the end of a course, and some want to keep in contact and fix a reunion date.

Depending on how long the group has been together and the nature of the course, there are activities to help learners 'let go' and move on. Learners write on a slip of paper what they have liked about another learner's contribution to the group. They do this for each person in the group. Learners are left with a pile of slips of paper with positive comments about their contribution to the group. We do not know how others see us much of the time, and some learners are quite emotional when they read that their peers think highly of them and have valued what they have brought to the group.

This gives a confidence to learners that they can take to their next group learning experience.

Teaching styles

The qualities learners value in teachers are fairness, not having favourites, being able to have a laugh without losing class control, being enthusiastic and knowledgeable about their subject, giving learners the confidence to think they can do well, and not giving up on learners.

The teaching style will vary according to the stage in the course and the group, and number of learners. A range of styles includes:

- *Autocratic*: authoritarian, 'do as I say', lion-taming (exerting discipline).
- *Telling*: giving out information or instructions.
- *Selling*: whipping up enthusiasm and interest.
- *Democratic*: negotiating, consulting, encouraging participation.
- *Facilitating*: acting as a catalyst and a resource.
- *Cultivating*: nurturing and developing the whole person.
- *Entertaining*: keeping interest through humour and unexpected resources or activities.

There are two styles that are counter-productive. The first is a laid-back, anything-goes, non-directional approach. Learners do not thrive with this type of teacher. I once suggested a teacher gave a group a team-building exercise to do. When I dropped by to check how the session was going I found him reading *The Times* and that the group had lost interest in the exercise. The second style is the teacher who makes themselves one of the group. Joining in is successful only if the teacher keeps a certain psychological distance. Learners do not want the teacher to be one of them. At the other end of the scale, learners are not comfortable if the teacher is psychologically too far removed from them, and therefore not easily approachable.

At the beginning of a course there is usually quite a bit of 'telling' and a certain amount of 'selling'. With a boisterous group an authoritarian style might be effective until the teacher feels they have control. Most learners enjoy an entertainer but not every teacher has the gift to be one. If it does not come naturally, it is better not to try because it will fall flat. When teaching one-to-one, probably a nurturing, democratic style will be the most appropriate.

Activity

This is an activity for the mourning/deforming stage of a group, when the course is coming to an end.

Think of a recent course you have been on. What would you have answered to the following questions?

1   What I will miss about this course
2   What I will not miss
3   What I am looking forward to when I leave the course
4   What I am not looking forward to

Reflection

How relevant is it to take an interest in the lives of your learners? What aspects of your own life would you be willing to share?

Professional Standards

This chapter relates to:

- Domain A: Professional values and practice
  AS4: Reflection and evaluation of their own practice and their continuing professional development as teachers
- Domain B: Learning and teaching

BS3: Communicating effectively and appropriately with learners to enhance learning
BS5: Using a range of learning resources to support learners.
Domain C: Specialist learning and teaching
CS2: Enthusing and motivating learners in own specialist area

Further reading and useful websites

Gravells, A. (2007) *Preparing to Teach in the Lifelong Learning Sector*. Exeter: Learning Matters.
Maslow, A.H. (1998) *Towards a Psychology of Being*, 3rd edn. New York: John Wiley.
Rogers, C.R. (1995) *A Way of Being*. Boston, MA: Houghton Mifflin.
Tuckman, B. (1965) Developmental sequence in small groups, *Psychological Bulletin*, 63, 384–99.

www.teachernet.gov.uk

7 Planning for individual needs

Something to think about: 'Fail to prepare and you prepare for failure'.

What this chapter is about

- Schemes of work
- Session plans
- Aims and objectives
- Teaching and learning activities
- Differentiation

Schemes of work

What is the difference between a scheme of work, a session plan, and session notes? A *scheme of work* is an overview of the content, aims and objectives, resources, activities, and assessments of a programme. I think of it as a skeleton. It is a working document, and I often put the content in a different order, or add different activities once I am delivering the sessions. I write the changes in pencil so that I can review what I thought I was going to do and what I actually did, and then I can rewrite the scheme for the next group of learners. *Session plans* go into more detail, giving structure to the session, with an introduction, development and conclusion, and adding the timings for each activity. Finally, *Session notes* are reminders to myself, for example which key points I must emphasize. They also act as an *aide-mémoire*.

Designing schemes of work can take time. But once the first draft is completed, making amendments for the next time the scheme is used is relatively quick. There are so many things to bear in mind, the first of which is the learners.

- Who are they?
- What is their age range?
- How many of them are there?
- What do they already know?
- Why are they on the programme?
- What are their interests?

All of the above will have a significant influence on the resources I choose. For instance, if I were delivering a programme on interview skills, I would make sure any

DVD I used was appropriate. It reduces the effectiveness of the DVD if adults are shown a DVD with teenagers being interviewed, or if young people wanting to get jobs in garages are shown a DVD of professional people applying for a management post. Finding the right resource can be a frustrating search and too often DVDs are shown and the teacher apologizes because it is dated or not quite fit for the purpose.

Although awarding bodies often stipulate what should be included in a scheme of work, I am usually free to select the activities I want. The topics for a scheme of work need to be in a logical order, and if there is an exam or test at the end, I will need to fit in some revision sessions. On some programmes, I include sessions on portfolio building. The number of sessions may again be dictated by the training organization. They, in turn, may be influenced by the amount of funding they receive for a programme. Some awarding bodies are prescriptive about the amount of class contact hours.

Assessments need to be spaced out so that learners are not overloaded with assignments. The skeleton plan enables one to see this at a glance. A further advantage of designing a scheme of work is that one has thought ahead about the resources needed, and one can book different rooms, TV monitors or guest speakers. Of course, should you fall ill or leave, the scheme is invaluable for anyone who takes your place. They know exactly what has been covered already and what needs to be delivered next.

Appendix 7 provides two examples of schemes of work that are quite different, although they are both about presentation skills. One is for a group of adult learners at a venue that is well resourced, the other for a group of young adults with limited resources.

The information from the scheme of work forms part of the session plan. A session plan should show the timings for each stage, the objectives, the resources, the teaching and learning activities, and the assessment. Therefore, the objectives, resources, and assessment can be transferred straight from the scheme of work. The teacher then only has to work out the structure, activities, and the timings.

Session plans

Everyone knows that first impressions are important, but how often do teachers launch straight into a session without any build-up? The introduction can lead to the success or failure of a session. It is very important to put some thought into the introduction. The aims of the introduction are as follows:

- to arouse interest;
- to empower learners so that they know what to expect from the session;
- to act as a link with a previous session;
- to establish what learners already know.

Learners become interested when:

- they know the purpose of the session;

- they are told what they will achieve by the end of the session;
- they are persuaded of the relevance of the topic for them.

Questioning learners, or using another activity, to determine what they remember from a previous session is good practice if there is a direct link between previous learning and the learning about to be undertaken. But it is also a way of consolidating learning, of promoting good feelings about learning, or of discovering they have remembered nothing of what you thought you had 'taught'! Young adults often say: 'We did that at school' or 'We've done this before'. When you say brightly, 'Good. So who can tell me what the function of the kidney is?', no-one can tell you. If it is material that they have covered before, ensure that the activities are fun and imaginative.

Never presume that learners have no previous knowledge of what you are about to teach. Always ask who knows anything about the topic. It does not matter if they do know, as you can draw on their experience. If the whole group says they have covered the topic before, unbeknownst to you, then you will have to do a quick re-adjustment of the structure of the session. One way is to put them in pairs or groups and ask them to set questions on the topic to ask the others. This way you will keep their interest and you will find out how much they really know.

How much leeway you have to choose the content of the session depends on the awarding body and the subject. Therefore, one accountancy course would most likely have the same content as another. But a qualification in teamwork skills could be achieved in many ways. I have observed young adults demonstrating teamwork skills through making films on a theme of their roots, designing a group sculpture, planning a visit or writing and producing an item for local radio.

A good conclusion rounds off the session in a planned way rather than vaguely ending and learners drifting off. In this way, learners can sense that there is a shape to the session, and that the conclusion plays a significant part in the learning. The conclusion can be used to:

- summarize the session;
- assess what has been learned;
- reflect on how learning can be applied;
- evaluate the session;
- provide guidance and motivation on how to develop the learning further;
- link to the next session by outlining what the content will be;
- set tasks based on the session.

Teachers should get in the habit of making brief notes on their session plans at the end of the session on what went well and what did not and what actions they need to take. If done straight away, it does not take more than a couple of minutes. It is also helpful to ask the learners what they enjoyed, what was difficult or tedious, and how they would like the sessions to be different. It is better to know the bad news so changes can be made.

It is generally thought desirable to have plenty of activities that involve learners, starting discussions and encouraging learners to think for themselves, and getting the information from the learners rather than the teacher doing all the talking. However, I remember an occasion when there were four teacher training groups, with a different course tutor for each group. To everyone's surprise, one group complained about the methods used. The tutor was renowned for his skill in playing devil's advocate and getting lively discussions going. His group wanted straight lectures. It was the way of teaching they were used to. I can only hope these trainee teachers used other methods as well as lecturing in their own teaching.

Aims and objectives

The difference between an aim and an objective can initially confuse, and to continue to confuse, trainee teachers. An 'AIM' is to do with the teacher's intention. An 'objective' or 'outcome' is what the learners will be able to do by the end of the session. It is through the assessment at the end that the teacher discovers whether the objective has been achieved.

A clue to sorting out if a statement is an aim or an objective is by looking at the verb. If the verb is vague, it is an aim. If it is specific and you can see how it could be assessed, then it is an objective. Appendix 8 provides lists of verbs to help you to write your aims and objectives.

'To give an introduction to first aid' is vague. How do you assess a statement like that? This is what the teacher's intention is. 'By the end of the session learners will have demonstrated the correct procedures for CPR (cardio-pulmonary resuscitation)' is much more specific. A teacher can easily assess if this objective has been achieved by observing the learners carrying out the task.

The sort of intentions a teacher might have include:

- To develop an understanding of ...
- To promote a positive attitude towards ...
- To develop skills in ...

The sort of outcomes a teacher might want at the end of a session are that the learners will be able to:

- correctly label a diagram of the heart;
- safely change a plug;
- list the ingredients to make a sponge cake.

When writing an objective, ask yourself if it is a SMART objective:

- Specific: Is it clearly defined, written in learner-friendly language?
- Measurable: Is it something that can easily be assessed? Does it take account of learners' ability?
- Achievable: Is it something the learners are capable of doing?
- Realistic: For example, do learners have access to the resources they need to achieve this objective? Is it suitable for the level of the programme?

- Timed: Does it give an indication of when the objective has to be achieved by?

Some objectives are difficult to measure, particularly in areas such as art appreciation or where feelings are involved. How can you assess if learners are empathic or have become less prejudiced?

In the following list, two aims are interspersed among four objectives. Can you spot the aims?

1 Recognize and correct the improper assembly of a child's car seat
2 State the main dangers to health and safety on a building site
3 Develop learners' confidence in speaking
4 Respond with personal feelings to the asylum issue
5 Equip learners with basic listening skills
6 Distinguish between snow, sleet, hailstones, and ice

(Numbers 3 and 5 are aims.)

Teaching and learning activities

When selecting methods or activities, it is important to consider the following:

- Are different learning styles catered for?
- What is being learned? A skill? Knowledge and understanding? A change in attitude?

We all have our preferred ways of learning. Teachers have to watch that they do not only use the methods that they themselves prefer. A simple way of finding out how people like to learn is to give them a list of methods and ask them to tick the ones they prefer.

There is a theory that some people are right-brain learners and others are left-brain learners.

Right-brain learners are visual learners and like to see the whole picture. They follow their intuition and tend to be imaginative and creative. Many dyslexic learners are right-brain learners. Teachers can help them learn effectively by:

- giving an overview of a new topic;
- showing learners what a finished product might look like;
- making use of mind maps and diagrams and pictures;
- letting learners decide for themselves how to tackle a task;
- giving plenty of examples and asking learners for examples of their own.

Left-brain learners, in contrast, are verbal learners who like to do one thing at a time in a logical order and are keen on the details. Teachers can help by:

- breaking learning down into steps or stages;
- making links explicit;
- giving learners rules to follow;
- using numbered lists;
- using texts or handouts.

The questionnaire in Appendix 9 will show you which you are.

Another model of learning styles is linked to Kolb's Learning Cycle. Kolb's theory is that for learning to take place, a learner should:

- have an experience;
- reflect on the experience;
- draw conclusions from the reflections;
- plan how to approach the experience a second time.

Honey and Mumford found that some people simply enjoy having new experiences. They are not reflective and do not learn from experience. These are the activists. Others engage in much mulling over what has occurred, but do not draw conclusions. They can be irritating, as they talk a lot about their experiences, often bemoaning what has happened, but are reluctant to think about why things turn out the way they do. These are the reflectors. The theorists, as the name implies, are full of theory, and have many explanations, but do not go on to change anything. Pragmatists are the sort of people who go on a training course and cannot wait to get back to work and try out new ideas.

In a learning environment, each of these types prefers certain teaching methods and dislikes others.

- *Activists* enjoy role play, games, and task groups and dislike lectures, reading alone, and very structured teaching.
- *Reflectors* prefer group discussions, case studies, and lectures and do not like being given tasks without being prepared for them.
- *Theorists* prefer lectures, demonstrations and are not keen on group work, especially when asked to explore their feelings.
- *Pragmatists* prefer demonstrations, coaching, projects, and work experience and dislike lectures and unstructured activities.

Appendix 10 provides a questionnaire for you to work out your own learning style. Learning styles can change depending on the work one is doing. Someone at university is likely to be a theorist, but become an activist if they move into employment where they are so rushed off their feet they have no time to reflect.

Although it is important to ensure teaching and learning activities are used that appeal to individual learning styles, at the same time learners need to be gently encouraged to develop the areas they score low in. This means building in time for reflection, drawing conclusions, and planning how to make changes.

A third model of learning styles is VAK or VARK. VARK stands for:

- <u>V</u>isual

- <u>A</u>ural
- <u>R</u>eading/writing
- <u>K</u>inaesthetic

The lesson from all three models is that teachers must use a mix of teaching and learning activities, and that if a learner is struggling, the teacher can help by using a medium that is more suited to that individual's learning style. For example, a *visual* learner may not be able to take in a lecture. They will need to have the information presented as a picture or demonstration. An *auditory* learner may not remember a silent demonstration. They need accompanying verbal explanation of what is happening. *Kinaesthetic* learners like hands-on experience. Learning will not fully have taken place until they have 'had a go'. *Read/write* learners need to put their thoughts down on paper, such as in a learning journal or writing an essay, and benefit from reading and discussing case studies and reading articles.

I had problems when attending an introduction to Urdu. The teacher said: 'My name is ... What is your name?' in Urdu and we had to repeat what she said, and then individually say it. I was unable to do this because I needed to see the words and write them down before I could make sense of them and remember them. The same thing happened when I started a Spanish class. Once the teacher put the sentences on the whiteboard, I had no further problems.

The learning styles of the individuals are not the only consideration. Different methods will be used depending on whether one is teaching a skill, knowledge and understanding, or changing an attitude. The most effective way to learn a skill is by:

- observing a demonstration;
- practising it;
- receiving coaching and feedback;
- question-and-answer.

Knowledge and understanding come about through:

- lectures
- question-and-answer
- projects

Attitudes are never changed through listening to lectures. In the Second World War, the American Government wanted housewives to start cooking offal such as liver, kidneys, and heart. They found lectures had no effect, but when people were put into discussion groups, their attitudes changed and they were more open to serving offal at meal-times.

Teachers often want to change attitudes to health and safety, presentation of work, or to other members of society. The most appropriate methods are:

- case studies
- discussion
- role play

Case studies are also useful for giving learners the opportunity to apply what they have learned. If they have been learning about discrimination, they could be given case studies and asked to discuss in small groups whether each was an example of discrimination, and if so, what type. If a teacher is comfortable with role plays, then the learners are more likely to respond well to them, although some learners may not enjoy them. They are useful for gaining an understanding of others as when learners role play being an elderly person in a care home. However, role plays need to be carefully prepared and the learners well briefed. Role plays can affect learners emotionally, so it is important to help them come out of role at the end.

Differentiation

It is difficult to plan sessions so that one caters for differences in ability and previous learning and motivation. Some session plans are designed to take account of differences. The objectives are worded so that the more able are stretched and the less able are given achievable goals. So there might be three objectives:

1   All must ...
2   Some may ...
3   A few might ...

Including 'open' tasks such as preparing for a presentation, designing a poster or preparing a dialogue gives learners the opportunity to work at their own level. Questions to individuals can be carefully selected to suit the ability, previous knowledge, confidence, and interests of the individual. Resources such as worksheets or reading materials can be individualized. (information and communication technology ICT) is invaluable for customizing resources. Size of print can be changed, background colour can be changed, and different images can be used.

New teachers benefit if they have a mentor. A mentor is a more experienced teacher, preferably in their subject area, who can act as a role model and pass on expert advice. All teachers, not just new ones, benefit from having colleagues with whom they can discuss their teaching. If there is a spirit of cooperation and sharing, teachers can observe each other's teaching and make suggestions. For instance, a teacher may ask another to come and observe them and suggest alternative activities. It is good practice to share new ideas and to share resources and even share session plans. Often a teacher will say: 'I hope you don't mind. I've stolen your idea'. If learners are going to benefit, then the more sharing that takes place the better. Anyway, teachers usually take someone else's idea and then adapt it to fit in with their own teaching approach.

Activity

Earlier in the chapter there was a section on aims and objectives. Test yourself to find out if you can recognize which of the following is an aim and which is an objective. The answers are listed at the end of the chapter.

1   Introduce learners to mime
2   Demonstrate five mime gestures
3   Evaluate own parenting style
4   Update on equal opportunity legislation
5   Increase awareness of effective parenting
6   State three examples of age discrimination

Reflection

'Fail to prepare and you prepare for failure'.

Have you ever been a learner when the teacher was not prepared? What were your feelings?

Have you ever been a learner when the teacher did not bother to adapt a session they had delivered many times before, to the needs of your group? This could be in the form of ancient notes, case studies unrelated to your interests, or teacher-centred methods such as lectures.

As a teacher, do you get satisfaction from planning a session and finding it has gone down well?

Professional standards

This chapter relates to:

- Domain B: Learning and teaching
  BS2: Applying an developing own professional skills to enable learners to achieve their goals.
  BS5: Using a range of learning resources to support learners.
- Domain C: Specialist learning and teaching
  CS4: Developing good practice in teaching in own specialist area.
- Domain D: Planning for learning
  DS1: Planning to promote equality, support diversity and to meet the aims and learning needs of learners

Further reading and useful websites

Cottrell, S. (2003) *The Study Skills Handbook*, 2nd edn. Basingstoke: Palgrave Study Guides.

Curzon, L.B. (2003) *Teaching in Further Education.* London: Continuum International Publishing Group.

Honey, P. and Mumford, A. (2006) *Learning Styles Questionnaire: 80 Items Version,* revised edn. Maidenhead: Peter Honey Publications.

Kolb, D.A. (1984) *Experiential Learning: Experience as the Source of Learning and Development.* London: Financial Times/Prentice-Hall.

Petty, G. (2004) *Teaching Today,* 3rd edn. Cheltenham: Nelson Thornes.

Rogers, J. (2007) *Adults Learning,* 5th edn. Maidenhead: McGraw Hill.

www.geoffpetty.com
www.vark-learn.com
www.peterhoney.com

Answers to the Activity

Numbers 2, 3, and 6 are objectives. Numbers 1, 4, and 5 are aims.

8   How much do they remember?

Something to think about: 'We forget to keep us from going insane'.

What this chapter is about

- What is memory?
- Remembering and forgetting
- Study skills

What is memory?

Memory is the ability to retain and recall information (Figure 8.1). As teachers, we need to plan how to help our learners remember. We are bombarded by information all the time, coming through all five senses. Stop and listen to all the noise around you, be aware of your body and any discomfort, pick up any smells, any residue tastes in your mouth, and look around and try and take in everything you see. Much of this we ignore most of the time. This is the *sensory stage*.

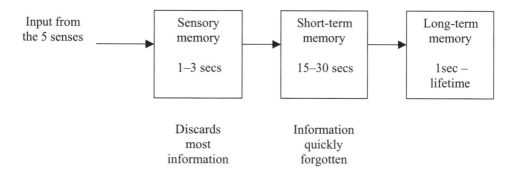

Figure 8.1   Model of memory

Only what is of interest to us or has got our attention is filtered through to the short-term memory. It is important for teachers, therefore, to get the interest and attention of learners. It has been stressed before that the introduction is vital for getting the interest of learners by explaining the relevance to them of what they are supposed to be learning. Making links with their own experiences and using resources and examples that appeal to their group will increase interest. Teachers can draw attention to key parts that need to be remembered by:

- using colour, underlining or capitals on the whiteboard;
- pausing and stressing key words;
- giving out handouts with key points bullet pointed;
- asking learners to summarize.

The *short-term* memory has a limited capacity and forgets very quickly. We cannot remember a string of numbers for more than a minute, and if there are too many numbers we are very unlikely to remember accurately. Once information has been processed from the short-term memory to the long-term memory there is little decay (decline). The main activities of the *long-term* memory are: storage, recall, and retrieval.

Teachers can help the *storage* process by using memorizing techniques. This involves thinking about what has to be memorized in a meaningful way and making associations.

- *Verbal association:* making up a story; linking things together; grouping things together.
- *Visual association:* draw a mind map with key words; put words inside drawings of objects; use different colours for different words.
- *Consolidation:* use the conclusion of the session to ask questions on what has been remembered.
- *Repetition:* read aloud, write out, record on tape, and repeat over and over again.
- *Frequent revision:* start each session with a quick quiz on the previous session; after a few weeks, give another short revision oral or written test.
- *First letter:* for example, SPERT is for Success, Purpose, Enjoyment, Reinforcement, Targets.
- *Rhyme:* everyone knows '30 days hath September …' Ask learners to make up their own rhymes to help them remember.

Appendix 4 contains an exercise that aids memory by making visual associations.

The other two activities of the long-term memory are recall and retrieval. *Recall* is when we know the answer without any prompting. 'Who was the mother of Queen Elizabeth 1st?' *Retrieval* is when we need cues, as with multiple-choice answers or true/false. 'The mother of Queen Elizabeth 1st was (a) Catherine of Aragon, (b) Anne Boleyn, (c) Queen Victoria, (d) Jane Seymour?' 'Anne Boleyn was the mother of Queen Elizabeth 1st. True or false?'

It is said that learners only remember the first and last ten minutes of a session. Therefore, it is important to bring out the key points in the introduction and conclusion of a session. There is a saying:

Tell them what you're going to tell them

- getting sidetracked on the internet
- writing lists

Learners often need guidance on how to approach writing assignments. It is helpful to give this advice when giving out the first assignment. It is best to give a written handout as well. The guidance might include:

- research and keeping notes on the sources;
- planning an introduction, main body and conclusion;
- using a spell and grammar check;
- referencing assignments (guidance on referencing is given in Appendix 5).

Learners are often worried that their work will not be what is required. There is only one way to allay fears, and that is by letting the teacher provide feedback. I usually set learners something to write early on in the programme. It may be a learning journal. Once learners have handed in one piece of work and received constructive feedback, they are not so reticent about giving in the next piece of work. Even so, some learners have such little faith in their ability that they need to be kept an eye on so that they do not fall behind with their assignments.

Activity

How do you best study? Answer the following questions:

- Do you study best in the morning/afternoon/evening?
- Do you like absolute quiet to study/music in the background/the television on?
- Do you prefer studying in short 20-minute bursts or for long periods of time?
- Where do you study the best: At home in the kitchen/living room/bedroom? At the training organization? In a library?

Reflection

What strategies do you use to remember:

- A car registration number?
- A credit card number?
- People's names at a large gathering?
- The ingredients for a recipe?

Professional standards

This chapter relates to:

- Domain B: Learning and teaching
  BS2: Applying and developing own professional skills to enable learners to achieve their goals
- Domain C: Specialist learning and teaching
  CS3: Fulfilling the statutory responsibilities associated with own specialist area of teaching
- Domain D: Planning for learning
  DS1: Planning to promote equality, support diversity and to meet the aims and learning needs of learners

Further reading and useful websites

Cottrell, S. (2003) *The Study Skills Handbook*, 2nd edn. Basingstoke: Palgrave Study Guides.

Wallace, S. (2007) *Teaching, Tutoring and Training in the Lifelong Learning Sector*. Exeter: Learning Matters.

www.bbc.co.uk/science/humanbody/mind

9 Assessment

Something to think about: 'If I find the work easy, I am not learning much'.

What this chapter is about

- Types of assessment
- Methods of assessment
- Assessment concepts
- Tutor, peer, and self-assessment
- Feedback
- Tutorials and reviews
- Record keeping

Types of assessment

Without assessment you will not know if anyone has learned anything. Assessment is crucial to every stage of a programme. You need to know what learners know already, how much they are learning during sessions, and whether, at the end, they have learned what you set out for them to learn. Assessment can be of knowledge, skills or attitudes and beliefs.

- *Initial assessment.* Learners are assessed formally or informally before starting a programme to ensure that they are on a programme that is at the right level for them, and one which will help them achieve their short- and long-term goals. This is also called *diagnostic assessment.* It is also good practice to check at the start of each session what the learners already know about the topic, by using question and answer or a short test.
- *Formative assessment.* Also called assessment for learning, this assessment takes place throughout sessions. Its purpose is to check learners' understanding and to enable learners to test their own understanding. In this way, teachers can determine whether they need to repeat part of the session or present it differently, before moving onto the next stage.
- *Summative assessment.* Also called assessment of learning, it establishes at the end of a session if the objectives have been met. At the end of a programme it is linked to qualifications; it is evidence towards the award of a certificate.

Assessing a learner before the start of a programme and comparing that with what the learner has achieved at the end enables teachers and others to judge how great a learner's progress has been. Assessment during the programme informs both teacher and learner on what headway the learner is making and identifies any problems in understanding. It should focus on how learners learn, not just on what they learn. A teacher can support a learner better if he or she understands how they learn, as it can give clues to why a learner is making mistakes. Final assessment moves more into the public domain, informing external bodies and employers of the achievements of the learner. However, some qualifications do not have a final assessment. Work done throughout the programme is submitted as evidence towards an award.

Nearly all assessment used to be *norm-referenced*, using marks, grades or rankings. This is where a group of people are judged against each other, resulting in a system where some people fail. Examples of this are the General Certificate in Secondary Education (GCSE) and Advanced (A) level exams. One of the purposes is so that universities, colleges, and employers can make selections. The 11+ exam is another example. Selective schools only want the top students to go to their schools. If they cream off the top 10 per cent, a child may be unfortunate if their year is a particularly bright one. In a system where there have to be failures, it can have lasting effects on those at the bottom.

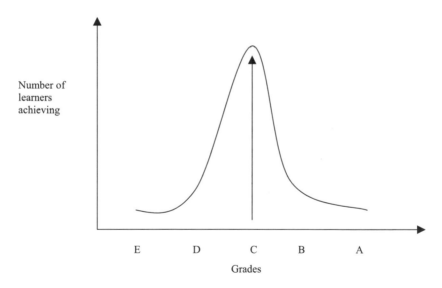

Figure 9.1 Curve of normal distribution

One year I was taking a group of motor mechanic students for Communication. The grades they got from me formed part of their overall grade as motor mechanics. These students had very good communication skills. They were persuasive and articulate, and individually and in teams performed well. I gave over half of them Distinction. The external verifier objected and wanted me to conform to the usual pattern of a very few getting Distinctions, some getting Merits, and most getting Passes. This is similar to the 'norms' in ordinary life with such things as height or weight or intelligence, where most people are in the middle (Figure 9.1). Russian is a subject where the 'norm' pattern is usually skewed (see Figure 9.2), because only students who are good at languages opt to take exams in Russian. As a result, most of them get 'A' grades.

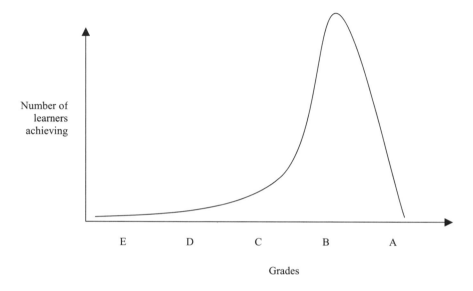

Figure 9.2 Skewed curve of distribution

Criterion-referenced assessment is where the learner is assessed against a standard. In theory, everyone attempting the assessment can achieve. Thus, if the criterion is 'Can make requests in French for food and drink in a café', then anyone demonstrating that skill will pass. An example of a criterion-referenced assessments is a National Vocational Qualification (NVQ)

Methods of assessment

Essays, exams, and tests are very formal methods of assessment. At the other end of the scale, quizzes, games, and question and answer are informal methods. Being assessed can cause learners to feel stressed. Therefore, whichever method is selected it is important to put learners at their ease so that they have the opportunity to perform to their optimum ability. They also need to be clearly briefed so that they understand what they are expected to do, including any time limits. Even if you have explained the assessment to them previously, learners appreciate it if the teacher recaps just before the start of the assessment.

Role play can cause confusion if the rules are not fully explained. For instance, if the learner playing the part of interviewer or counsellor is the one being assessed, the 'client' needs to understand that it is their responsibility to give the interviewer the chance to show their skills. Sometimes the 'client' gets caught up being such a difficult or loquacious individual that the learner cannot meet the assessment criteria.

Where possible, learners should be given the option of the medium in which they present their evidence. One learner may be more comfortable doing a poster or designing a booklet. Another may prefer to give an oral presentation. Many learners prefer doing on-line tests rather than handwritten tests.

Case studies are useful for assessing knowledge and understanding as well as attitudes and beliefs. However, if they form part of a small group discussion, it is difficult to judge as one individual may contribute more than the rest. The same applies to group projects.

Essays are easy to set but time-consuming to assess. Multiple-choice tests take time to design but are very quick to mark. They can also be marked by non-experts. Once you have written a multiple-choice test, it is there to use again and again. Of course, you will not know if a correct answer from a learner is a pure guess. This applies even more to true/false questions, where there is a 50 per cent chance of getting the answer right. Some e-line tests, when they are multiple-choice, may not really test if a learner can, say, calculate the area of a room, because they are only guessing at an answer and do not have to work out the calculation. Learners enjoy writing multiple-choice questions for each other. They pose a question and give three or five possible answers. One answer is usually obviously wrong.

Question: Where is the carotid artery?

1   In the foot?
2   In the neck?
3   In the rabbit's hutch?

Assessment concepts

When selecting an assessment, it is important to check if it is:

- valid
- authentic
- reliable

A certain teacher's aim is 'To change learners' eating habits'. The objective for one session is 'State the reasons for eating a balanced diet'. The assessment brief is 'Go into town and compare the prices of pizzas and pasta meals'. For an assessment to be *valid*, it has to test what is supposed to be tested. In this case, it is clearly not testing whether learners know the reasons for a balanced diet. Some people argue that intelligence tests do not test intelligence, as they are often culture-based, and people can be coached into getting higher marks. Marking a learner down for poor grammar, or for what they are wearing, when it is not relevant to the assessment, also affects the validity. Be clear what the criteria are and only assess these. Sending learners off on a task away from where they can be observed, or getting them to work on an assessment in pairs or groups, can raise questions of *authenticity*. How does the teacher know it is the learner's own work? Maybe by comparing the standard of work with what the learner produces in class. Or by asking supplementary questions.

Reliability is related to fairness. The conditions should be exactly the same for each assessment, whoever is taking the assessment and whoever is assessing. Therefore, learners need access to the same resources, and the same amount of time to complete the assignment. The criteria must also be the same every time the test is given.

Currency is relevant in some cases. A First Aid certificate only lasts for a limited time and then the training and assessment has to be repeated. Many qualifications only last a set number of years. A learner may be able to produce a spreadsheet in one session, but will have forgotten how to do one the next week. They will need to be assessed on more than one occasion. How many times is sufficient to be confident that a learner is competent at a task? That will depend on the task, and the learner.

Tutor, peer, and self-assessment

Most of the time, the teacher is the assessor. But there are benefits to using the learners' peers to undertake the assessment, as well as from learners assessing themselves. Being assessed can be a passive activity. It relies on the judgements of others rather than forming one's own opinion, and being responsible for one's own learning. Getting learners to assess themselves develops their independence and makes them more motivated. However, self-assessment skills need to be learned. And there are emotional reactions to confronting what one is not doing so well. Many learners become upset when they find learning difficult or do not succeed first time. They become negative and their response is: 'I can't'.

The learning process involves:

- making mistakes;
- struggling to understand;
- having to ask for help.

These are good signs. They show that learning is happening.

Teachers need to get learners to view the learning process in a positive way. Finding something challenging is an opportunity to learn something new. It is natural to make errors, and we all can learn from making mistakes. When someone first tries to ride a bicycle, they wobble and fall off a few times. All learning is like that. It is okay to make mistakes. This gives learners confidence and reassurance in not always being right.

Learners can be taught to assess *what* they have learned. They need to know what the session objectives were and then they can identify what new knowledge, understanding, and/or skills they have acquired. They can also be taught to assess *how* they learned. To do this they need to identify:

- what really made them think;
- what they found difficult;
- changes to the session that would have made learning easier for them;
- what they would like more help with.

From this, the learner can plan what they are going to do to improve. Throughout, the teacher will be giving feedback and support.

Peer assessment

Using peer assessment develops learners' analytical and communication skills. Learners tend to judge someone else's efforts as 'good', 'average' or 'weak'. With practice, they can qualify their judgements with reasons and specific examples. They also learn to assess with sensitivity and in a constructive way. Assessing a peer's work leads to making comparisons with one's own work. Being more critical about one's own work, recognizing strengths and weaknesses, builds up self-esteem, and gives pointers to areas that can be improved upon.

Sometimes peers are too 'kind' when assessing, maybe because they want others to be kind to them in turn, or because they are assessing a friend. The teacher has to explain why honest feedback is more helpful in the long run than only praise. Feedback from peers can sometimes mean more to a learner than feedback from the teacher. In Maslow's hierarchy, respect from others was a basic need. Learners want the respect from their fellow learners.

Peer assessment can be used in different ways:

- Exchanging short answer tests with a partner, and marking the test as the teacher and class discuss the answers. The learner will be able to compare the answer they gave and will inevitably work out who is right if the answers differ.
- When everyone has produced something such as a flower arrangement, a model or a pictorial presentation, peers can be asked to comment. *The teacher must always remind learners to make their comments constructive.*
- When learners demonstrate a skill, peers can check what was performed correctly and what was not. Learners need to have a list of criteria to look for.
- Peer assessment is useful when learners give presentations, as a range of opinions is helpful. One person may find the pace too fast, another that they could not see the screen from where they were sitting, another appreciate the use of colour.
- Where learners are practising guidance, advice or counselling, three of them may be involved, taking the roles of an interviewer, a 'client', and an

observer. The observer will assess from an observing role. The 'client' will assess from a more subjective view. The 'interviewer' will self-assess. Again, the criteria must be made clear.

Feedback

Feedback can be oral or written. Whichever form it is in, it should be remembered that the purpose of feedback is:

- to motivate and encourage;
- to give praise where due;
- to give one or two suggestions for improvement.

Feedback is often given in a form of a 'sandwich', with examples of what was good, one or two negatives, and ending with an overall positive summary.

I am often asked: 'What do you do if there is a lot to criticize?' If a learner receives an overwhelming amount of criticism, they are going to feel a failure and quite likely they are going to give up trying. Remember that when one is starting out on learning something new, it is common to do a lot wrong. The teacher should prioritize. Health and Safety issues would come top of the list for changes the learner should make.

Some people say they only want to hear what they are doing wrong and do not need to have the praise for what they are doing well. These are usually people who anticipate that there is, in fact, little that they are doing wrong. When they experience a long list of negatives and no praise, they invariably find it an unpleasant experience. Even if they are that very rare breed who can take a lot of negative criticism, they should not presume others are like that.

Comments such as 'excellent', 'good' or 'disappointing' are not helpful. Learners want to know why their work is excellent, or what they have done that makes their work disappointing. Similarly, just a tick or cross, a mark out of ten or a grade does not tell a learner how to improve. Comments should be specific, related to the criteria, and if given by peers it should be made clear that it is a personal opinion. An example of peer feedback is as follows:

> Your talk was well-structured and the visual aids were amusing and original. If I was giving the presentation I would have used a black marker pen instead of a yellow one, because I think black is easier to see from the back of the room. However, you made a very persuasive case for giving up the car and taking to the bicycle.

Feedback should be given as soon as possible after the event. This applies to written feedback as well. If the gap between event and feedback is too wide, the impact is lost.

People differ in their opinions about where feedback should be written, and how, and what colours to use. Some recoil from writing on learners' work. Personally, I often write in the margins and at the end of a piece of work. I also design feedback sheets for my written comments. Whether to put rings around spelling mistakes, punctuation errors, and grammatical inaccuracies depends on the importance of all these to the qualification or subject being studied. On teacher training courses, if the learner's English is weak, I correct it. On an interpersonal skills course, I would ignore any mistakes. Similarly, with young adults who have previously rejected learning, I would want to encourage any efforts, and leave corrections until a later date.

Red pens have connotations with school, so many teachers avoid using them. One needs to find a way of distinguishing the feedback from the learner's work. Some teachers use pencil or a blue pen if the learner has used a black one.

Tutorials and reviews

Tutorials and reviews are opportunities to discuss progress with the learner privately. And the discussions of both need to recorded, with copies for both teacher and learner. Tutorials are usually for feedback on assignments. One or two tutorials may be timetabled into a programme for each learner or they may take place when a learner requests a tutorial. Reviews are usually once every six weeks or so and are often used when learning is work-based, and an assessor visits the workplace but is not themselves based there. (Some learners may need to be visited more frequently, for shorter reviews, if they have a learning difficulty.)

Tutorials and reviews need to be structured, with a beginning, a middle, and an end. The teacher should explain the purpose and the format, such as: 'The tutorial is to discuss the first draft of your assignment. I'll give you feedback and then you can ask any questions', or 'We have half an hour for our review of your progress. I am going to ask you first about how well your work is going and any difficulties you are having. I will then give you some feedback on your progress, as I see it, and then we will agree an action plan. Do you have any questions before we start?' The end should summarize the tutorial or review.

It would be unfair to wait until the end of a programme to inform a learner that they are not suited to further learning or employment in the area they have been studying. Giving feedback on progress throughout the programme gives the opportunity for a teacher to raise any serious concerns they are having about a learner's suitability, so that the learner is not taken by surprise as the programme is ending.

It can be uncomfortable to be the bearer of bad news. Sometimes the learners themselves have a growing awareness that their skills and ability do not match up with the requirements for their chosen learning or employment path. The teacher can find out what the learner is struggling with or not enjoying. I asked a trainee learner, who had not established any rapport with his groups, whether teaching was living up to his expectations. He answered: 'I'm not really enjoying teaching practice. My groups don't listen to me and they keep saying they don't understand. They don't seem interested'. I suggested that he might be more suited to giving talks about a subject that he knew well, rather than facilitating learning. We agreed to review the situation later, by which point he had concluded that he was not suited to teaching.

A learner on a counselling programme was causing grave concern. They had unresolved personal issues that intruded into the classroom practice. Whatever 'problem' they were listening to in role plays, they summarized back to the 'client' that the client's mother had not given them love, and launched into telling the client what they were feeling and why. I raised my concerns during tutorials. The learner reacted aggressively.

However sensitive one tries to be, there will always be one or two learners who will react defensively, and sometimes unpleasantly, to feedback. All the teacher can do is base the feedback on agreed criteria, and remain rational and calm. They should keep a written record of what took place in case there are further repercussions.

Record keeping

Records need to be kept of:

- *Learners' progress:* This is so the teacher can keep check of what has been achieved and what is still to be done. It also can be used if the learner leaves half way through or if a new teacher has to take over the class.
- *Achievements:* This is so that the organization knows who has completed, and for quality assurance, where external agencies want to know the achievement rates.
- *Feedback from assignments, tutorials, and reviews:* This is to provide evidence that thorough assessment and support has taken place

---

Activity

Read these comments on learners' work. How constructive are they? How could they be improved?

1 Well done! You're maintaining your high standard of work.
2 You have fully met the criteria.
3 A well-structured essay.
4 Full marks.
5 You have covered several important health and safety issues. What measures could be taken to ensure visitors do not infect patients?
6 You have covered all the questions correctly except for Q2. Look again at the handout on the heart.
7 You answered interview questions confidently. You need to watch your body language.
8 Check your spelling on your CV. Change 'Yours sincerely' to 'Yours faithfully' on your letter of application. Re-do the application form in black ink.
9 An imaginative poster with plenty of appeal for young people. The choice of colours works well.
10 See me at the end of class.

Reflection

Is it true, do you think, that if learning is too easy, then not much is being learned? Do people vary in the amount of challenge they are comfortable with? Is learning more exciting if it is challenging? Should learning start off easy and become more challenging later?

Professional standards

This chapter relates to:

- Domain B: Learning and teaching
  BS3: Communicating effectively and appropriately with learners to enhance learning
- Domain D: Planning for learning
  DS2: Learner participation in the planning of learning
- Domain E: Assessment for learning
  ES1: Designing and using assessment as a tool for learning and progression
  ES2: Assessing the work of learners in a fair and equitable manner
  ES4: Using feedback as a tool for learning and progression
  ES5: Working within the systems and quality requirements of the organization in relation to assessment and monitoring of learner progress

Further reading and useful websites

Tummons, J. (2007) *Assessing Learning in the Lifelong Learning Sector*, 2nd edn. Exeter: Learning Matters.

www.aaia.org.uk
www.slamnet.org.uk/assessment
www.qca.org.uk

10 Evaluating learning – involving the learners

Something to think about: Statistics may not always give the whole picture. It is easy to jump to conclusions in the following examples.

Teacher A starts off with 18 learners. All but six leave before the end of the programme. The remaining six are entered for an exam and get 'A' grades.

Teacher B starts off with 15 learners. Fourteen learners are still on the programme at the end. Of the 14 entered for the exam, ten pass with 'C' grades.

What this chapter is about

- The place of evaluation in the 'training cycle'
- Reflective practice
- Involving learners in evaluation
- Who sees the evaluations
- What happens next

The place of evaluation in the 'training cycle'

The training cycle consists of a teacher:

- identifying learners' needs;
- planning and designing learning;
- delivering learning;
- assessing learning;
- evaluating teaching and learning.

Evaluation plays a significant part in the cycle, if it is carried out thoroughly. Everyone involved in the process needs to take it seriously. The purpose of evaluation is to:

- provide feedback on learners' learning and achievement;
- provide feedback on the quality of teaching and support;

- use the information to make improvements in the content, design, and delivery of the programme.

Evaluation is either quantitative or qualitative.

Quantitative evaluation, using numbers or percentages, enables one to compare and contrast, for instance:

- learners' retention rates;
- achievement rates;
- attendance/absences;
- progression to further learning;
- progression to employment.

Retention is important, not only because it may be related to funding, but because if learners are voting with their feet, it is a sign that either they have been directed to the wrong programme or the teacher is not keeping their interest.

Some programmes get funding according to how many learners achieved qualifications. Learners, however, may want to stay on the programme but do not want or need a certificate, so do not submit the required assignments or sit the required tests. I recall a programme called 'Setting up your own business'. The learners were very keen to get all the information they needed from the teacher but not only were they not interested in getting a certificate, they feared that if anyone other than the teacher – such as internal and external verifiers – saw their ideas, they might copy them! Verifiers, of course, are bound by professional ethics, so this would not happen.

The support the learner received might affect retention, achievement, attendance, and progression. Therefore, the quality of the programme needs to be evaluated.

Qualitative evaluation is more subjective. It is to do with the learners' perceptions, the teacher's self-evaluation, and the observations of the teachers' colleagues or verifiers.

Reflective practice

The quality of teaching will not improve over time unless the teacher is engaged in self-evaluation. It is said that if self-evaluation does not occur, a teacher with 20 years' experience may be teaching in the same way as when they started, making the same mistakes, and very likely using the same session plans.

Reflective practice is a state of mind, involving constant self-evaluation. Kolb's Learning Cycle applies to teachers as much as to learners. Delivering a session is an experience, we reflect on it, we draw conclusions, and finally we plan what to do next session.

Donald Schön identified two types of reflection:

- *Reflection-in-action:* changes you make on the spot. During the session you might realize that something is not working and hastily make adaptations, or get a brainwave about something extra you could introduce or a better way of presenting something.

- *Reflection-on-action:* reflections you have at the end of the session. It is good practice to make a note at the bottom of the session plan on what went well, what did not, and what changes you will make next time you deliver that session

Teachers should also reflect on the support they are giving individual learners. It is too easy to teach to the whole group and not notice that one or two learners are losing a little motivation or seem less committed to their learning, which could be because of the teaching or for external reasons that could be picked up upon. Signs to look out for are non-attendance, lateness, being behind with assignments, and tension when asked questions.

Involving learners in evaluation

It is usual, on short courses, for learners to be handed out evaluation forms to complete at the end of the day or the course. People are ready to go home and may feel the forms are a waste of time and that no-one other than the teacher will see them.

The way in which the forms are handed out can influence how motivated the learners are to put some thought into their responses. Often a teacher will say, 'Would you fill in the evaluation form at the back of your pack before you go'. The learners hastily scribble their answers, which could be as brief as: 'OK', 'Liked everything', or they often leave out questions altogether. Or the teacher may say, 'If you haven't time to fill in the evaluation form now, would you send it in to me later'. The percentage of learners posting back their replies will probably be low.

How much more effective it would be to leave time at the end of the day and say, 'I've left the last ten minutes for you to give me feedback on the course. I'd really appreciate your honest comments on what has been useful for you and what I could do to improve the course. I do read what you say and do make changes as a result of feedback from groups'. This sends the message that filling in evaluation forms is worth the while spending thought and time.

Some teachers ask learners to evaluate at the end of each session, particularly if learners are in class for a half day or whole day at a time. Others ask the learners to evaluate mid-way and at the end of a programme. Some only get evaluations at the end. This is a bit too late to do anything for the current learners, which is why an added evaluation mid-programme is a good idea.

Learners are sometimes reluctant to be honest with their evaluations. They know that even if they do not have to put their name on the forms, the teacher will know their handwriting and be able to identify them. I was on a programme as a learner and I found myself looking to see how the people either side of me had rated the teacher. I thought the teacher was below average, but when I saw the others had written 'Excellent', I upgraded my rating to 'Good'. I still feel ashamed of myself for not being honest, but I remember that occasion when I am trying to encourage my own learners to be honest. Otherwise, the exercise is a pointless one.

When the group is small, the teacher can leave the room so that the learners can discuss their feedback on their own, and then one of the group can give a summary of their conclusions when the teacher returns.

An informal way for learners to evaluate is to write a series of statements with 'smiley' faces underneath. Each learner circles the face showing their level of satisfaction for each statement (Figure 10.1). Another informal way is to hand out post-its in different colours. Each learner writes on the pink post-its what they found enjoyable and on the blue post-its what they least enjoyed. They then stick the post-its on two pieces of flipchart paper and everyone can read what everyone else wrote.

Figure 10.1 Smiley faces for evaluating programmes

Questions with a choice of answers from 1 to 5, or from 'Excellent' to 'Poor', are quick to fill in and can inform the teacher to a certain extent. There are two problems with these, however. I have known learners who do not read the instructions and think '1' is the best rating and '5' the worst, so that every aspect of the programme is rated at rock bottom. The other problem is that if several people have given the content a poor rating, you have no idea what they would have liked included or what they would have liked omitted.

Open questions take more time to fill in but provide better information for the teacher to act upon. As this is time consuming, it is better to restrict oneself to asking fewer questions that can be fitted on to one page. Such questions might include: 'What have you found most useful?' and 'Which activities did you most enjoy?'

What aspects of a programme should be evaluated by the learners? The organization is often interested in knowing learners' opinions on:

- pre-course information
- pre-course advice and guidance
- crèche provision
- refreshment provision

Teachers want to know learners' opinions on:

- the content
- the resources
- the activities
- the teacher's delivery
- the support given

There is often only one question on support. A more searching set of questions needs to be asked if the teacher is going to gain anything from the answers. Learners can be asked about the quality of support they received:

- *on the first day* – listening to any anxieties, answering queries, giving information on the programme;
- *during class sessions* – encouraging, motivating and coaching, and meeting individual needs;
- *in tutorials* – giving time for the learner to raise their own issues;
- *at the end* – giving advice and guidance on progression to further education, training or employment.

The best way to get answers is in discussion with the learner. This would take too long with even a medium-sized group, so if possible the discussion could be incorporated into a tutorial.

Who sees the evaluations

If the teacher is working for themselves, then maybe the only other people to see the evaluations, or a summary of them, might be prospective new learners or organizations interested in using the teacher for training. Usually, many more people are involved. Within the organization it might be:

- other team members
- the team leader
- the internal verifier
- the managers

External to the organization it might be:

- the external verifier for the awarding body
- employers
- inspection teams such as the Office for Standards in Education, Children's Services and Skills (Ofsted)
- funding bodies

All these groups might also be involved in carrying out evaluation of their own. External employers often ask their employees to evaluate the training course they have been on, identifying what they have learned and how it can be applied in the workplace. Team members, verifiers, and inspectors may observe a teaching session, and write a report.

What happens next

There is a suspicion that evaluation goes into a filing cabinet to be forgotten. As with all the evidence gathered at initial assessment, what happens next needs to be tracked and recorded.

Usually there is a team meeting. The evaluations by the teacher, the internal verifier, the external verifier, the learners, and anyone else involved are discussed and an action plan is drawn up, identifying who is responsible for carrying out the action and by when. It is important that the action plan is monitored at a later meeting. In this way, there is more chance that changes and improvements will be made.

Finally, it is motivating for people praised in evaluations to get to hear about it. At one college, the librarians were consistently mentioned by the learners for their helpfulness and friendliness. At another college, the learners were effusive about the delicious lunches provided. In both cases I made sure the staff concerned had copies of the evaluations.

Activity

Which of the following do you think is important in a teacher? How would you rate yourself?

- Sense of humour
- Enjoys and respects learners
- Enthusiastic about subject
- Knowledgeable about subject
- Someone learners can talk to
- Knows each learner individually
- Fair-minded
- Manages behaviour well
- Motivating
- Creative
- Makes learners think they can do well
- Does not give up on learners

Reflection

Read again 'Something to think about' at the beginning of the chapter.

1   The retention rate of learners with Teacher A is 33 per cent. What question(s) would you need to ask to discover the reason?
2   Is the information on retention and achievement related to Teacher B qualitative or quantitative evaluation?

(Answers to the questions are listed at the end of the chapter.)

Professional standards

This chapter relates to:

- Domain A: Professional values and practice
  AS4: Reflection and evaluation of their own practice and their continuing professional development as teachers
  AS5: Collaboration with other individuals, groups and/or organizations with a legitimate interest in the progress and development of learners
  AS7: Improving the quality of their practice
- Domain D: Planning for learning
  DS3: Evaluation of own effectiveness in planning learning

Answers to 'Reflection' questions

1. Ask for reasons for withdrawal from the programme. The learners may have left because they have found employment. If, on the other hand, the reason is not known, then the remaining learners' evaluations may give a clue. Observation of the teacher's delivery could also explain the drop-out rate.
2. Quantitative evaluation.

Further reading

Kolb, D.A. (1984) *Experiential Learning: Experience as the Source of Learning and Development.* London: Financial Times/Prentice-Hall.
Moon, J. (2006) *Learning Journals.* London: Routledge.
Schön, D. (1991) *The Reflective Practitioner.* Aldershot: Ashgate.

11 Communicating – what message are they getting?

Something to think about: 'Never assume communication has taken place'.

What this chapter is about

- The sender and the receiver
- Technical terms and jargon
- Teacher talk
- Questioning technique
- Voice and speech
- Body language

The sender and the receiver

Communicating is a skill that we need to work on throughout our lives. Because it is a two-way process, we need to consider not only how we are communicating but whether the message is being received in the way we intended by the person or persons on the receiving end.

I had a sociology teacher who was extraordinarily fluent and could talk at us for hours but I only had a hazy idea what he was talking about. I got left behind wondering what his sociology terms meant while he carried on in full flood. A teacher with a strong accent or one who has distracting mannerisms can create barriers to the message getting through to the learners. For myself, I have sometimes given what I think are crystal-clear briefings before an activity, and the learners look confused or misunderstood the task. Emotions can get in the way. A learner may not take in everything the teacher says or may misinterpret what is being said if they are over-anxious, or if they are resistant to the ideas being put forward. Background noise, visual distractions or the learner's own thoughts intruding, all can act as barriers to communication.

Albert Mehrabian found that when someone is trying to communicate with us where feelings are involved, and the actual words are incongruent with the tone of voice and body language, then we are more inclined to believe the message we are getting from tone and body than the words. In fact, he concluded that we get

38 per cent of the real message from tone of voice and 55 per cent from body language. As an example, a teacher could say, 'If you have any questions, come and ask me', and say it in a hurried way as they turn away to scoop their books into a briefcase and put their coat on. The message the learners get from the body language is that the teacher wants to get away fast. The throwaway tone of voice sends the message that the teacher is hoping no-one will ask questions. Feelings and attitudes are revealed through non-verbal communication.

Teachers need to be on the look out for non-verbal behaviour that is incongruent with what the learner is saying. A learner says, 'I *promise*, I did do my homework but I left it on the bus'. If this is said with forced emphasis and the learner avoids eye contact, it is worth probing deeper. If the learner has not done the homework, then is it because it was too difficult, because the learner is not planning their study effectively, or are there extra pressures at home at the moment?

Learners are helped when teachers:

- present new information in plain English;
- define technical terms and acronyms;
- give easy-to-follow demonstrations;
- explain tasks unambiguously;
- ask questions in a way that helps them in their understanding;
- speak audibly, using the voice to arouse and maintain interest;
- communicate non-verbally to create a rapport;
- listen to them.

Technical terms and jargon

Every subject has its specialist terms and abbreviations. This can be bewildering for a learner new to the subject. On the radio, if an interviewee uses an unfamiliar term or abbreviation, the interviewer will interrupt and ask: 'What does that mean?', 'What does that stand for?' Learners tend not to ask, and are left in the dark.

In education at the present time, many words are reduced to initials:

- QTLS: Qualified Teachers – Learning and Skills Framework
- PTLLS: Preparing to Teach in the Lifelong Learning Sector
- CDP: Continuing Professional Development
- DIUS: Department for Innovation, Universities, and Skills

When I am observing teachers practising in a diverse range of subjects, I am still bemused by the number of specialized words that are apparently necessary. Who would have thought that the everyday act of shampooing hair could involve hand movements with names such as 'effleurage' and 'petrissage'. Information technology courses are a minefield of terms and abbreviations, which appear even in beginners' self-help books:

- PDF: Portable Document Format

- HTML: HyperText Markup Language
- Defragmentation
- Trojan

It is useful to look at all the words that might be unfamiliar to your students and to highlight any that you might use in your session notes. This will remind you to stop and write up the term and explain it. If the word is going to be used again, leave the word on the whiteboard or wherever it is written as a reminder to the learners. At the start of the next session, ask if they remember what the word means or what the abbreviations stand for. You could ask them to keep a note of new words, or you could give them a glossary of words they are going to come across. Learners will not remember new terms by having them explained only once.

If there is a more common alternative for the word, then make the association for the learners. Bloom's Taxonomy of Objectives is divided into three Domains: Psychomotor, Cognitive, and Affective. At the introductory level of teacher training, learners find these words and terms difficult to remember, so I use simple, familiar words with a similar meaning: 'type' for Domain, 'skill' for Psychomotor, 'knowledge and understanding' for Cognitive, and 'feelings and attitudes' for Affective. I also break down words such as 'Psychomotor' by asking what 'psycho' could mean (of the mind) and what 'motor' means in this context (relating to movement or muscular activity). There are many words that can be broken down to decode their meaning.

Teacher talk

Teachers lecture, explain, demonstrate, and question. Some tend to talk too much. One of the values of planning sessions is that you can look at the proportion of time you are doing the talking compared with your learner or learners. Listening to a lecture is not the most effective way of learning. Figure 11.1 shows that learners gain more from being actively involved than from passively receiving information.

Lectures, or giving information, have a place, but they should be broken up with activities involving the learners. Some ways of doing this include:

- giving the learners a problem to solve;
- asking them to form pairs and share the notes they have made;
- giving them a few multiple-choice questions to answer;
- asking them to discuss, in small groups, what you have said so far;
- asking them to write down a question they want to ask;
- asking pairs to write down the key points of the lecture so far.

For maximum effectiveness, *demonstrations*, with an accompanying explanation, should be followed immediately afterwards by learners having a practice. Or, the teacher can give a silent demonstration and then ask the learners to watch closely as they will be asked questions afterwards. The teacher can give a demonstration and then repeat it, but ask questions such as the following:

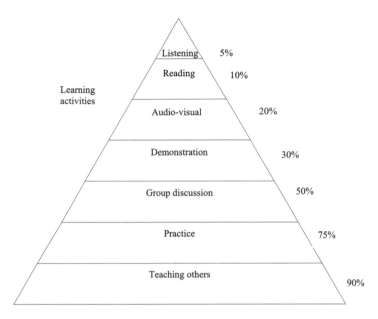

Figure 11.1 Learning pyramid showing that it is more effective to learn by applying new knowledge than by listening or watching

- What did I do first?
- What did I do next?
- Why did I do this in this way?
- What would have happened if I had done this instead of this?

This is effective in making the learners think for themselves. Alternatively, the teacher could give a demonstration and ask one learner to repeat it and ask the others to spot if there are any mistakes.

Demonstrations should be very well prepared. You should:

- *Analyse the sequence of steps.* When a skill is very familiar to you, you are likely to leave out crucial steps, because they have become second nature to you.
- *Practise it* once or twice so you do not leave out a key action or explanation.
- *Make a list* of everything you will need for the demonstration. This is useful not only to do a last minute check but when you give the demonstration again to another group. It looks less than professional if you realize in the middle of a demonstration that you have left a resource at home.
- *Check all the equipment* is working before the start of the session.
- *Arrange the room* before the learners come in and set out the equipment you will be using.

When giving the demonstration:

- *Check everyone can see* before you start.

- *Stress the key points*, either by slowing down or pausing.
- Stress any health and safety points.
- *Link your actions to theory.* Explain *why* you are doing something in a certain way. Learners remember more readily when they understand the reasons behind what they are doing.
- *Keep to a logical order*, and do not backtrack.

After the demonstration, you should;

- Give all learners the opportunity to practise
- Observe them and coach and give feedback.

Questioning techniques

Teachers ask questions throughout a session. In the introduction they question to establish what learners remember from a previous session, or to establish if they know anything about the topic about to be introduced. Questions at the start of a programme are often asked to create a rapport with learners and to put them at ease.

During the session, teachers ask questions to check how much the learners are understanding. Questions are useful for getting the attention of those who look as if they are falling asleep or who have become distracted. They are also asked to increase learners' confidence, to draw on their experience, and to provoke discussion. During the conclusion of the session, questions are used to assess learning or to consolidate learning.

It is more stressful to be questioned on a fact, where there is a right or wrong answer, than to be questioned on one's opinion. 'What is the date of the Battle of Waterloo?' raises the heart rate more than being asked 'Do you agree with abortion?' This is worth remembering with unconfident learners. It can be more comfortable to answer questions on facts *after* discussing them with a partner.

Inexperienced teachers often do not give learners time to think of the answers. They rush to fill the silence by moving on to another learner for the answer, or quite often they give the answer themselves. While it might appear that nothing is happening in the silence, the learners are actually thinking about their replies. There is a technique of asking questions known as:

- Pose – a question
- Pause
- Pounce

Pausing after posing a question is good practice. The 'pounce' sounds rather intimidating. I interpret 'pounce' as selecting an appropriate learner to answer – for example, an easy question for an unconfident learner and a more demanding one for a more able learner. By choosing someone to answer, the teacher can make sure everyone gets to give an answer. At the same time, the teacher needs to create an atmosphere where the learner is not put down if their answer is incorrect. There are ways of responding to a wrong or partly wrong answer. 'You're not quite on the right track' can be followed up by a further question that gives the learner a clue. 'No, but a good try' will not discourage the learner from answering future questions.

There should be a mix of questions:

- *Closed* questions, where there is a right or wrong answer. (What are the names of the bones in the arm?)
- *Open* questions. (What are the benefits to society of diversity?)
- Low-level questions asking for *facts*.
- Higher-level questions requiring *reason*. (What would be the result if bread was made without yeast?)

Some questions can be prepared beforehand and written into the session plan. Others arise as a result of what is happening during the session. Whether prepared or not, questions should be:

- brief
- unambiguous
- simply worded
- related to one point

Voice and speech

Whether a teacher speaks with a regional accent or with a foreign accent does not matter as long as they can be heard and understood by their learners. It is hard, however, to listen for long to speakers whose voices are monotonous or grating or to speakers who have irritating speech mannerisms.

If a group of learners are talking among themselves, speaking quietly sometimes works much better than shouting. The learners have to stop talking to hear what the teacher is saying. Shouting above the noise of learners just adds to the commotion. Added to that, some teachers, in particular women, tend to become shrill when they shout. Varying the volume keeps the interest of the learners.

Voices can be improved by relaxation, posture, breathing, and opening the mouth! Tension affects the voice, so easing the shoulders and neck before speaking helps relaxation. Standing or sitting up straight gives the rib cage and diaphragm room to expand and let air in. Too many people try to talk without breathing and this creates tension and, again, some people barely open their mouths when they speak. Try taking in a deep breath and humming 'Mmmmmmmmm' and then open the mouth to 'Ahhhhh'. Immediately the voice is projected, and can be heard clearly at the back of a room.

People think nothing of exercising the body or doing warm-ups, but they often think it strange to exercise the voice. Yet the voice and speech benefit as much as the rest of the body from exercise. The following exercises improve resonance and projection. The voice can be used to arouse interest, to get attention, to calm a group down, to get a laugh. This is done by varying the pitch, pace, volume, and the use of stress and pause.

Try the following exercises, varying the volume and tone for each sentence (Remember to relax and sit up straight and take in slow, deep breaths):

- Shout louder. I can't hear you with this wind.
- Shhh. You'll wake the baby.
- Help, someone. I can't open the bathroom door.
- Miss Jones is wearing a wig.

It is difficult to listen to someone who talks at the same pace for any length of time. The following exercise gives practice in varying the pace and tone:

Drip, drip,
Trickle, trickle, trickle,
Splash,
Ooze,
Spatter, spatter, spatter,
Squelch, squelch,
Surge.

It helps learners to pay attention to key points if they are stressed. This can be done by writing them on the whiteboard, or underlining them in a handout, but also by *vocal stressing*. With these next exercises, stress different words to get different meanings. For instance, in the first sentence, try stressing the word 'touch' and the next time you say the sentence, stress 'dare'.

- Don't you dare touch me
- Where are you going?
- No, don't do that
- Take it off
- Isn't he clever?
- What have you got in there?

Poor articulation results in words getting lost and, particularly if you are talking to a large group of people, they will find it difficult to hear what you are saying. The following exercises give practice in sounding consonants. Do not forget the importance of vocal projection – that is, *consciously* directing the voice to the back of the room without shouting.

- Each sixth chick sat on a stick
- I bought a box of biscuits, a box of mixed biscuits, and biscuits-mixed
- Truly rural
- Fetch me the finest French-fried freshest fish that Finney fries
- Which wily wizard wished wicked wishes for Willy?

- She stood on the balcony, inexplicably mimicking him hiccupping, and welcoming him in

Appendix 14 is a choral poem that is fun to do and which develops an expressive voice.

Body language

Does appearance matter in a teacher? I think so. First impressions are important, and we all make assumptions about others when we first meet them. I dress quite differently according to the subject and the learners. If I was running a session on presentation skills to managers, I would be dressed in a smart suit. I tend to wear floaty skirts when running counselling courses. As an external moderator, when I am visiting programmes for disadvantaged groups, I do not want to stick out as a visiting 'official', because I want to interact with them informally and hear what they really think of their learning provision. Some teachers can get away with being scruffy, but they usually have a special charisma. At the other extreme, a teacher can appear unapproachable if dressed too formally.

Whether to stand, sit on a chair or sit on a desk? Whether to stand still at the front of a class or move around the classroom? It is a matter of personal preference, but it is valuable to think about what style you are using and reflect on what message it is sending and whether it is the one you want to send. It is useful to move around because it keeps the attention of the learners. Standing indicates that you want to be leading at that moment. If you then sit down, it sends out a signal that you want the learners to be more involved, and for them to initiate discussion. When learners are busy on a task, I often kneel down beside them or draw up a chair, because I do not want to be looming over them when I look at what they are doing. Some people stand in front of a class and take one step forward and then one step back, or shift from hip to hip, reflecting an unease with being the focus of attention. These movements have no purpose and are distracting for the learners. Perching on a table controls such unconscious mannerisms.

As teachers we have to be careful not to make assumptions about our learners. Learners of all ages can create the wrong impression. One learner may come to the first session as timid as a mouse, not speaking, head down. Another comes in very cocky and loud-mouthed. Another behaves aggressively at the first session. As teachers we must look beyond the body language and get to the real person underneath, or the public persona will be reinforced.

We need to pick up messages from learners' body language when they are in need of help in some way. A slumped body may only be as a result of a late night; on the other hand, it may be a sign of despondency. Sometimes a learner will try and hide what they are writing so no-one else can see. It could be that they are struggling. There are theories about what scratching the nose or crossing the arms mean, but they are unhelpful. The best way to read body language is to observe an individual and discover the unique things they do when they are being defensive, experiencing anxiety, feeling aggressive, and so on. Behind a smile may lie sadness, duplicity, deviousness, insincerity, as well as pleasure or a welcome.

Activity

How clear are your explanations? Describe the shape below to a partner and see if they can draw an identical shape.

Figure 11.2

Reflection

- How do you feel about the way you speak?
- How could you communicate more effectively?

Professional standards

This chapter relates to:

- Domain A: Professional values and practice
  AS4: Reflection and evaluation of their own practice and their continuing professional development as teachers
  AS7: Improving the quality of their practice
- Domain B: Learning and teaching
  BS3: Communicating effectively and appropriately with learners to enhance learning

Further reading and useful websites

Anderson, R.W., Krathwohl, D.R., Airasian, P.W., Cruickshank, K.A., Mayer, R.E., Pintrich, P.R. *et al.* (eds) (2001) *A Taxonomy for Learning, Teaching and Assessment: A Revision of Bloom's Taxonomy of Educational Objectives.* New York: Addison Wesley Longman.

Mehrabian, A. (2007) *Nonverbal Communication.* Piscataway, NJ: Aldine Transaction.

Ridge, J. (2002) *The Complete Voice and Speech Workout.* New York: Applause Theatre Book Publishers.

http://en.wikipedia.org/wiki/albert_mehrabian

12   Personal problems

Something to think about: 'The more a person is understood and accepted, the more he tends to drop the false fronts with which he has been meeting life and the more he tends to move in a direction which is forward' (Carl Rogers).

What this chapter is about

- Personal problems and boundaries
- Listening and responding
- Helping learners make changes
- Challenging negative thinking
- Referring learners

Personal problems and boundaries

Personal problems can interfere with learning. It is hard to concentrate when you are upset or worried about something in your private life. Having someone to talk it over with can be very helpful. However, the responses you get can be irritating or leave you no nearer knowing how to solve the problem.

Friends tend to take your side or to give advice, and tell you what you should do, you must do, you have to do. Generally, people do not take advice because they feel half-hearted about the suggested solution. Carl Rogers noticed that, providing you listen to others and give them space to think aloud, they will come up with their own solutions and because the solutions are their own they will be more motivated to take action than if they were following someone else's advice.

This sounds simple, but being a good listener is a difficult skill to acquire. How many people find it easy to listen without interruption and to refrain from giving advice? How many people jump to the solution instead of giving the other person the space to express their feelings? We often have an urge to sort people out in a bossy, if well-intentioned way.

Personal problems with an emotional content will rarely be solved unless the person can first give vent to their feelings and have them acknowledged. It is only then that they are in a fit state to look for ways out of the problem.

Teachers are not trained counsellors and should not attempt to counsel. What they can do, however, is to use counselling skills, sometimes called *listening skills*, to help learners to help themselves. *Counselling* involves a formal contract and an explicit relationship where one person is the client and the other is the counsellor. *Counselling skills*, however, can be used to enhance one's work role. The purpose is to help learners to help themselves. As with formal counselling, confidentiality is essential, providing if it is within the requirements of the law and one's own contract of employment. (Prisons, for example, require teachers to pass on certain information, but the learner inmates would be aware of this.) If it is necessary, or it would be helpful, to discuss a learner's problem with a colleague, or in a wider team, then the learner must either provide their consent or the teacher must give a valid reason why confidentiality is being broken. Gossiping about learners' private matters would be unethical.

Teachers, having listened to a learner's concerns, must then make a series of judgements:

- *Is this problem outside the teacher's expertise?* In which case, the learner should be referred.
- *Is the problem outside the teacher's professional role?* With a disadvantaged group, helping learners with their problems may be part of the teachers' role. On some programmes, learners are expected to use the organization's student services or counselling service as the first port of call.
- *What are the time constraints?* If a session is just about to start, then the teacher can ask the learner to wait until the break or until the end of the session. If the teacher senses that the learner is going to need more time than the teacher has to spare, then they can refer the learner. On rare occasions, the problem might be of such urgency that the teacher has to delay the start of a session, but this should only be in very unusual circumstances. (I can think of an occasion when a learner arrived straight from witnessing a bad traffic accident. They were in a state of shock and it seemed appropriate to let them tell the whole class what they had seen. I then suggested they went off with a friend for a cup of coffee.)

The teacher must always be careful of their own motives, and not fall into the trap of either giving up so much free time that they exhaust themselves, or that they get seduced by the pleasure of rescuing others.

Listening and responding

Carl Rogers said that the quality of the relationship between the learner and teacher, and the attitudes and personal characteristics of the teacher, were of utmost importance. He said that the teacher should:

- *Be genuine.* By this, he means being one's real self and not acting a role. It means being open and approachable and not putting up defences. A learner will then feel it is safe to show their real self. Being genuine is the most difficult of qualities to develop, and one which others will see through if you only act being genuine.

- *Feel and demonstrate empathy.* Empathy should not be confused with sympathy. Sympathy is feeling sorry or feeling compassion for another person. Empathy is the ability to place yourself in another person's shoes for long enough to sense what life is like for them. You can never feel exactly as someone else, even if you have had the same experience Therefore, saying 'I know just how you feel' cannot be true. It is helpful to filter the content of what you hear into two bags – yours and the learners. For example, take the statements 'My aunt is dead' and 'My cat is dead'. If you have experienced an aunt or a cat dying, you relate to what is being said. However, if you mix up your experiences with those of the speaker, you are in danger of assuming that their emotions are the same as your's were. Your relationship with your aunt may have been remote and her death did not have any great effect on you. The speaker may have been very close to her aunt and may have been devastated by her death. I once had a learner on a counselling skills course who said they could not take it seriously when their 'client's' concern was their grief over their dead cat. This learner could not empathize.

- *Be accepting.* This is about valuing and respecting the learner as a human being of worth. It is about not giving up on a learner because of their behaviour, or being judgemental about the life choices they make. In this way, the learner will experience being valued unconditionally for what they are. When someone else has unconditional regard for us, we begin to like ourselves a little bit more.

Carl Rogers refers to these as 'a way of being'. By this he means that being genuine, the ability to feel empathy, and valuing and respecting others are part of how one is all the time, not qualities that are turned on and off like a tap.

It is important to recognize the value of being listened to and being 'heard'. We often feel that no-one understands how we feel or the situation we are in. The first step is for the teacher to let the learner tell their story without intruding. Giving all of one's attention to the learner, and showing you are listening by using speech fillers – nodding from time to time or saying 'yes', 'um' – is all that is needed. The next step is to paraphrase in your own words what you think you have heard. This has two purposes. First, it shows the learner that you understand not only the key points of their story but that you understand how the learner is feeling. Second, if you have misunderstood anything, it gives the learner the opportunity to correct you. For example, the teacher might say 'You're really angry with the mugger', and the learner might say 'No, I'm more frightened what my partner will do when he finds out the money has gone'.

There are many instances when the learner will feel a bit better once they have told someone else what personal upset or distress they are experiencing. 'A trouble shared is a trouble halved' is often true. The communication between teacher and learner can be quite brief. It is not up to the teacher to solve the learner's problems. However, it can mean that the learner feels calm enough to give their attention to the lesson. Some teachers ask everyone to unload the 'baggage' they have come in with (worries on their mind) to the rest of the group at the start of the session.

Personal problems are usually to do with loss of some sort. People become distressed by the loss of a ring or a diary because of their significance. Relationships change, inevitably: people split up, children leave home, illness affects the dynamics of a relationship, and people die. Changes in life are often, although not always, unsettling. It is helpful to understand the effects of different types of change and how different personalities react.

Some people see change as an opportunity, and some see change as a threat. If you look at change as: 'As one door closes, another opens', then life is less difficult for you, as you can let go of the past and look forward to the future. Others fight and kick and resist every change that comes along. If you accept change easily, then it may be hard to understand those who are fearful or who grumble. Nothing in life stays the same, as change is part of the human condition, so helping learners to cope more positively with change is important.

We will have more negative feelings about changes that are imposed upon us than changes we choose to make, although there will always be a period of adjustment. Similarly, we will have stronger emotional responses to changes that are of a more personal nature. Therefore, if a learner is evicted from a home they do not want to leave, the emotional response is going to be more negative than if they choose to move house, and the more support they are going to need from those around them.

Learners can get very upset when there are changes within the learning programme. If a new teacher takes over the programme mid-way through, it needs to be handled with care. It helps if learners can air their feelings and anxieties straight away. The sooner this is done, the sooner they will settle down.

Sometimes a group will be moved to a different room for one or two sessions. This can also give rise to grumbles. Because the change is imposed, the learners may feel they are of no consequence in the organization, and they feel hurt and angry. To the teacher, familiar with the setting, this may seem an extreme reaction. If the reason for the change is explained, and the inconvenience of it acknowledged, then the learners are more likely to accept it. On the other hand, if the teacher also feels pushed about by the organization and conveys this to the learners, then the level of discontent will rise.

Death is something many would rather avoid talking about. Yet the process of grieving involves coming to terms with the loss, and this is helped by being able to go over the events again and again. Also, there is an awkward atmosphere if no-one mentions the death. When a learner returns to class after a death, it may be helpful to speak to them privately and say, 'I'm sorry to hear about ... Do you want to talk about what happened?' This leaves the learner with the choice of whether or not to tell the teacher. If the learner wants to describe what took place, then it will not take more than a few minutes, and the teacher can then invite the learner to discuss later what future sessions he or she will need to miss, and so on.

When you accept that it is not your responsibility to solve other people's personal problems, it is easier to listen to others. All that is required is to show that you have understood, by reflecting back the content and the feelings. Making judgemental comments or giving advice is unhelpful. What is appropriate, in some circumstances, is to offer to give the learner information on how they can seek specialist help, or to offer to arrange a referral, if that is within the teacher's role.

Because talking about a concern is so therapeutic, the teacher needs to ensure that they do not inadvertently interfere with the learner's flow. The learner should be allowed to talk about what they want to talk about. It is tempting to interrupt the flow with questions asking for facts ('How many times did that happen?') or for reasons ('Why did you allow that to happen?'). With these sort of closed questions the direction of the story is dictated by the listener instead of the learner, and after a time the learner will wait for a question before talking. Open questions or tentative statements are more effective. 'Where would you like to start?', 'It sounds as if you are becoming resentful'.

Helping learners make changes

To help learners make changes, teachers can guide them to resolve the problem through a series of questions:

- What is the problem?
- What outcome do you want?
- What ideas have you got that might achieve that outcome?
- What are the pros and cons of each option?
- Which option is the best?
- What steps do you now need to take?

This is effective if the problem is something that is within the learner's power to change. For example, a learner does not know how they are going to get to class for the next month because their car has broken down and they cannot afford to get it mended.

- *What is the desired outcome*? To have some means of transport. (It is surprising how many people find it hard to identify what it is they want. Without clear goals, problems remain problems and do not get solved.)
- *What are the possible options*? Getting a lift, getting public transport, borrowing someone else's car, borrowing money to get the car mended or using a bicycle.
- *What are the advantages and disadvantages of each option*? An advantage of getting a lift might be that one could save up money to get the repairs done. A limitation might be that the person giving the lift does not go home at the same time. Using a bicycle might have the advantage of providing independence but the limitation might be that it would be difficult to transport portfolios and textbooks at the same time. The reason it is essential to think through each option is so that the limitations are recognized before the final choice is made. Otherwise, the solution may end in failure and the learner will be back to square one. Planning how to put

the option into operation also needs careful thought. The learner needs to identify the sequence of steps they need to take and when they are going to take them.

- *Action planning.* If the choice was to borrow someone else's car, the steps might be to make a list of people to ask, to put them in order of those most likely to agree, to prepare a persuasive request, to visit the first person on the list that evening and, if turned down, to visit the next person on the list. Plans can fail when the details of each step are not worked out. The learner will tend to put other priorities first such as going out with friends, and a week will go by without anything being achieved.

A teacher can guide a learner through the sequence quite quickly. Sometimes the part that takes the longest is finding out what the learner really wants. Equipping learners with the skills to solve their own problems helps them become more responsible for themselves and more in control of their lives.

Challenging negative thinking

Why do people hold themselves back? Often we are our own worst enemies. We decide something is impossible and instantly it becomes impossible. But:

- Can a man with no legs run?
- Can a man who can't speak or move achieve scientific greatness?
- Can a woman who is deaf become a professional musician?

Oscar Pistorius, who is a double amputee, competes in Para Olympics running races; Stephen Hawking, who is severely disabled with a neurological disease, writes books on science; Evelyn Glennie, who is deaf, is a professional percussionist.

Negative thinking keeps people stuck. It deprives them of so many new experiences and achievements. Some negative statements include:

- I'm not clever enough
- I'm no good at exams
- They won't consider me – I'm too young
- They won't consider me – I'm too old
- I know I won't get it right
- I'm going to forget what to say
- I didn't get accepted this time, so I'll never get accepted
- I can't do maths
- Everything's stacked against me
- I never complete a course

The negative thinker will jump in and argue, 'It's true, some people aren't good at exams', 'Employers aren't interested in anyone over 40', 'You've got to be realistic about what your strengths and weaknesses are'. The point about negative thinking is that it affects one's feelings and behaviour. It results in giving up before one has started, because the outcome is already certain.

There are three ways a teacher can help learners who have negative attitudes about themselves. One way is to challenge their statements and another is to build up their confidence, and the last is to encourage them to have dreams and aim high.

Negative talk tends to consist of generalizations or seeing a catastrophe where there is none. Teachers can ask questions that show up faulty thinking.

- You say you can't do maths. Can you cut a cake into eight pieces? Can you work out how much weight you have lost or gained? Can you fill in your pay claim?
- What do you mean by everything is stacked against you? Do you mean that because there have been one or two setbacks it is now impossible for you to succeed?
- It is normal, wouldn't you say, to feel nervous when you are giving a presentation? And it's normal to be worried about forgetting what to say, but you know you have your prompt cards. And what is the worst that can happen if you need to look at your notes?

Having belief in a learner is a great boost to their confidence. As is giving them opportunities for small regular successes. Added to this, the teacher needs to remind the learner that they are succeeding, so they do not drop back into an old pattern of thinking negatively about themselves. And because patterns are engrained, negative thinking is not stamped out overnight.

The better the relationship a teacher has with a learner, the more influential they will be in helping the learner believe in themselves, take risks, and change things. And the more likely it will be that the learner accepts the challenge from the teacher to see themselves or their situation in a new way.

Referring learners

Time constraints and lack of expertise mean that learners with personal problems will need to be referred in many instances. Referrals are not always managed well, and the learner is left without support. Teachers should weigh up how much they themselves should be involved. Sometimes it is enough to hand out a leaflet or give a contact name, in the knowledge that the learner can cope on their own and that the referral will be straightforward.

Unfortunately, some agencies only work on certain days at certain hours and have to use a voicemail in lieu of a receptionist. It can be frustrating trying to arrange an interview. Personnel come and go, and the information the teacher has could be out of date. The learner may give up in disappointment. Many counselling agencies have waiting lists. Teachers should pre-warn learners if this is the case.

Learners in a vulnerable state may feel unable to make contact themselves and would prefer the teacher to do it for them and explain the situation, and even go with them to the agency. There is a balance between stepping in appropriately and being over-supportive. When a learner has suffered a traumatic experience, then they need, for a time, others to make decisions for them. If the teacher is the person arranging an interview, they should get permission from the learner about how much information to divulge. It is even better if the learner can listen in on the conversation the teacher has with the agency. And once the referral has been made, the teacher must let go. They are no longer involved. However, they should check that the referral has occurred and that the learner is satisfied.

Teachers come across more learners with personal problems because of the diversity of their groups. There could be problems of addictions, relationship breakdowns, pregnancy, homelessness, sexually transmitted disease, domestic violence, debt, and feeling suicidal. A teacher can feel overwhelmed and out of their depth if they are suddenly approached for help. Knowing to whom to refer the learner enables the teacher to manage the situation in a professional manner. Thus it is advisable to keep a file of leaflets and local agencies that offer help.

Activity

Over the next week, try this exercise with three different people on three different occasions:

- Listen without interruption (if you are on a mobile, instead of face to face, you will need to give the odd 'um' so the person the other end knows you are still there)
- Do not offer advice

What were the results? How difficult did you find it? Are you as good a listener as you thought you were? What have you learned about yourself?

(This exercise works best when you are listening to someone complaining about something or someone.)

Reflection

- Are you good at keeping confidences within your family group? What has happened in your family if someone has broken a confidence?
- How difficult do you find it to keep confidences at work? What are the problems?

Professional standards

This chapter relates to:

- Domain A: Professional values and practice
  AS4: Equality, diversity and inclusion in relation to learners, the workforce and the community

AS5: Collaboration with other individuals, groups and/or organizations with a legitimate interest in the progress and development of learners
- Domain B: Learning and teaching
  BS2: Applying and developing own professional skills to enable learners to achieve their goals
  BS4: Collaboration with colleagues to support the needs of learners.
- Domain F: Access and progression
  FS2: Provide support for learners within the boundaries of the teacher role

Further reading and useful websites

McLeod, J. (2007) *Counselling Skills*. Maidenhead: McGraw-Hill.
Mearns, D. and Thorne, B. (2007) *Person-Centred Counselling in Action*. London: Sage Publications.
Rogers, C.R. (1995) *A Way of Being*. Boston, MA: Houghton Mifflin.
Sanders, P. (2002) *First Steps in Counselling*. Ross-on-Wye: PCCS Books.

www.addaction.org.uk
www.citizensadvice.org.uk
www.connexions-direct.com
www.samaritans.org
womensaid.org.uk

13   Behavioural problems

Something to think about: When learners misbehave, they do it to achieve a goal.

What this chapter is about

- When is behaviour a problem?
- The purpose behind problem behaviour
- I'm OK – You're OK
- Minimizing problem behaviour
- Transactional analysis
- Bullying
- Developing interpersonal and intrapersonal intelligences

When is behaviour a problem?

Learners cannot learn if one or more are behaving in a way that disrupts the whole class. This is grossly unfair. Teachers have a responsibility to do something about disruptions, for the sake of their learners. Of course, it is annoying for the teachers themselves when they cannot get on with a session, but they should be thinking first and foremost about the effect bad behaviour is having on the other learners. Examples of disruptive behaviour include:

- talking to others when the teacher is speaking;
- shouting out;
- making rude comments about other learners or the teacher;
- throwing bits of paper, drink cans, etc;
- swearing;
- shoving other learners.

Teachers can unwittingly create disruption by the way they respond to such undesirable behaviour as refusal to work or provocative comments to wind the teacher up. And the behaviour of mature learners can also annoy the others and disrupt their learning. Common behaviours include:

- regularly turning up late for class;

- dominating discussions;
- airing their complaints during class time;
- demanding special attention;
- sulking;
- claiming to be superior to everyone else.

Some behaviour is undesirable even though it is not disruptive. Because such behaviour does not annoy the teacher as much, these learners are sometimes left alone when it would be more helpful for them if the teacher addressed their behaviour. Such behaviour includes:

- 'switching off' – making no effort to join in;
- reading mobile texts;
- looking at written tasks but not starting them.

Learners need supportive strategies on the part of the teacher so that their behaviour no longer gets in the way of them learning.

The purpose behind problem behaviour

The purpose behind much problem behaviour is to attract attention. Consequently, if the teacher gives the learner a lot of attention, the learner's goal is achieved. If a learner craves to be noticed, there are other more constructive ways a teacher can give them attention. Ignoring undesirable behaviour and redirecting it and then praising behaviour you want repeated is better.

It should not be surprising if learners are tempted to liven things up when a session is very boring. Active minds need stimulation and if the teacher has not made the content and activities interesting, then the learners will find ways of injecting some excitement. The solution lies almost entirely in the hands of the teacher.

Some learners have a chip on their shoulder and feel society, education or teachers have given them a raw deal. Their goal is to pay people back, so they attack psychologically or physically. Building up a relationship where there is trust and respect may take time but it usually stops the problem behaviour. If the behaviour has become bullying, then the situation is more serious.

Others are motivated by a desire to control. They like an audience to witness the confrontations they have with the teacher. It therefore reduces the satisfaction the learner gets if the teacher addresses the challenges to their authority in a more private setting. Having a confrontation in front of the whole class may well encourage the learner to carry on challenging.

Many learners misbehave to avoid failure. They fear they will find the activities in the class difficult – answering questions, doing worksheets, undertaking practical tasks. Rather than ask for help or face up to the fact that we do not always get things right first time, they do not even attempt to do their work. This may be compounded if they have difficulties with basic reading and writing skills. They feel helpless and hopeless. Discouragement like this can only be reversed by encouragement from the teacher, giving small achievable tasks and changing negative thinking

I'm OK – You're OK

Thomas Harris described healthy adults' emotional attitude to life as 'Life is worth living – let's live it to the full'. He called this 'I'm OK – You're OK'. This is an adult who is confident in themselves and respects others.

Some learners carry with them less healthy emotional attitudes to life, relating to their early experiences as children. In addition, even healthy adults will fall back on one of these attitudes if they feel anxious, threatened or powerless. You might recognize times of stress when you adopt one of the following positions:

- I'm not OK – You're OK. This person lacks belief in themselves. They have no confidence that they can achieve. They compare themselves unfavourably with others. Building up their confidence and giving them achievable tasks can change this attitude.
- I'm OK – You're not OK. This is an emotionally defensive position as a result of being hurt in the past. The person gets a feeling of self-worth from being a survivor, and telling themselves that others do not matter and they can do without them. Most teachers have come across learners who are hostile to them or fellow peers. It is important not to mirror their hostility. Rather, the teacher needs to act as a model, valuing and respecting the learner as a unique human being.
- I'm not OK – You're not OK. This is a very bleak attitude to life. It does not matter what we do or who we hurt because there is no hope in life. Clearly, this is an extreme view but can be the view of those who have been neglected, abused or unloved as children. Teachers who have very diverse groups may meet learners with this attitude. An understanding of this may enable teachers to support such learners.

Minimizing problem behaviour

When the learners like and respect the teacher and sessions are varied, relevant, and enjoyable, unwanted behaviour is very much reduced. If the teacher does not work at building relationships with learners who might be disruptive and/or disengaged from the learning process, then other strategies are less likely to be effective. From the start, the teacher needs to get to know each learner as an individual, and to be aware of factors in their personal lives that may affect their learning. The teacher needs to build up a mutual respect through being fair and consistent, and ensuring there are times when they and the learner are communicating one-to-one and the learner feels they are being listened to.

Bill Rogers states that in addition to the relationship between teacher and learner, certain steps can be taken to pre-empt misbehaviour. I would put it the other way around – misbehaviour, or restlessness at the very least, will surely follow if you do not take the following steps:

- create well-structured sessions using a variety of activities;
- set up the classroom before the session starts and check resources;
- provide content and tasks relevant to learners and which are pitched at the right level;
- introduce extra activities for learners who finish quickly;
- provide sufficient time during the session for some individual support for learners who need it.

This is common sense, but it means planning and preparing thoroughly. Recycling old session plans without adapting them to a particular group, not taking into account individual needs, or not giving oneself enough time to set up before the learners arrive is asking for trouble.

If problem behaviour occurs in spite of having a good relationship with a learner and having designed a good session, then the way a teacher responds can escalate the problem. Over-reacting, shouting, sarcasm, and humiliating a learner will not achieve your goal. A calm, rational approach is more effective. The learner can be reminded of the ground rules and the sanctions for infringing them. If the learner is angry, then it is even more vital to remain calm and to ask the learner to explain why they are angry. As in the previous chapter, it is important to communicate that you have heard what they feel and think, so one needs to summarize and clarify what has been said. Only then can one look at solutions.

Teachers who mete out a lot of punishment may cause learners not only to dislike and fear them, but also to hate the subject. Learners can become immune to punishment if they receive it too often. Learners may not like the punishment but it still may not stop them carrying on misbehaving. They may enjoy misbehaving more than they dislike being punished!

Giving less attention to minor misbehaviour, or not making a big issue of it, is preferable in the long run. Where possible, it is effective to distract the learner, redirect them to the task they are supposed to be doing, or remind them that they can have a break once they have completed their work.

I observed one teacher who was much admired and liked by his groups. The learners arrived with very poor records of behaviour from their schools. He rarely had any problems with them. When a new learner joined the group, they would, at first, follow their usual behaviour, such as defacing their worksheets and not doing any writing. The teacher would ignore the learner (and so would the rest of the group). In a very short time the learner would start engaging in the session and joining in with the others.

Transactional analysis

Eric Berne said that human beings are hungry for recognition, preferably in a positive form such as approving comments and friendly exchanges. He called these 'strokes'.

This need is so basic to us that if we are being ignored, we will seek negative strokes (such as being shouted at or even hit) from others, by behaving badly, because any recognition is better than none. Wherever this may have originated – for example, from parents or teachers who only took notice of the child when they were being naughty – it can become a habit, so that the learner deliberately sets out to attract negative strokes whatever environment they are in.

As all behaviour is learned (we are not born being well behaved or badly behaved), teachers can modify behaviour by rewarding behaviour they want to see repeated, and withdrawing rewards for undesirable behaviour. Learners like being praised and having positive notice taken of them. They do not respond to being treated like a child, especially when they approach the teacher in an adult manner.

Eric Berne's transactional analysis model of the three tapes, or ego states, can be very enlightening, showing teachers how they are unwittingly communicating with learners in ways that escalate problems. The three tapes – Parent, Adult, and Child – are tapes we automatically start playing when we are communicating with others. We all catch ourselves using the same phrases our mother or father used with us, such as 'Clear up this mess' or 'Don't worry, I'll sort it out for you'. When we find ourselves in similar situations, we start our Parent tape. If we had a very critical parent, then that is the tape we will use more when learners are not doing what we want them to. Others will draw more on their Nurturing Parent tape. With this tape we make responses that are caring and may tip over into being indulgent.

The Child tape is either Free Child or Adaptive Child. We start off life as a natural or free child. We do not want to lose this part of ourselves. It is the side of us that is spontaneous, fun-loving, and creative. However, we soon learn that we cannot be as free as we would like, and we learn to adapt. Some children become very compliant, eager to please their parents. Others react by becoming rebellious. Others find they can still get their own way by being manipulative. In later life, they draw on these tapes.

As teachers we can encourage the Free Child by planning enjoyable activities and engaging in shared humour. When a joke is shared, both learners and teacher are communicating using their Free Child tapes. But we need to be careful how we respond when learners use their Adaptive Child tapes. We need to recognize that when a learner accuses us of picking on them, that they want us to get cross and use our Critical Parent tape. Using the Adult tape is usually more effective. The Adult tape is our mature, rational self. Learners, like teachers, use a mixture of tapes, and this is only a problem if one of the tapes is used inappropriately, leading to anger or hurt or resentment.

Figures 13.1 and 13.2 provide examples of exchanges, which Berne calls transactions, between learners and teachers. A reciprocal transaction is where the responder replies using the same tapes as the speaker. A crossed transaction is where the responder replies using different tapes.

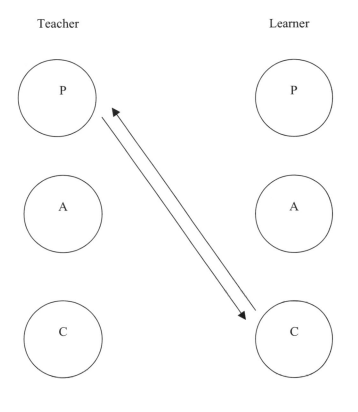

Teacher (Critical Parent)   "You've done nothing but cause
To Learner (Rebellious Child):   trouble all morning."

Learner (Rebellious Child)   "Well, that's because your
To Teacher (Critical Parent):   lessons are a waste of time"

Figure 13.1 Reciprocal transaction

Bullying

Bullying, or harassment, causes so much misery and fear. It may take place in the classroom or during break times, but increasingly bullies are using mobile phones and the internet. Teachers need to be supportive by giving advice when learners are bullied outside of the learning environment. The emotional stress of being bullied affects all of one's life, including interfering with learning.

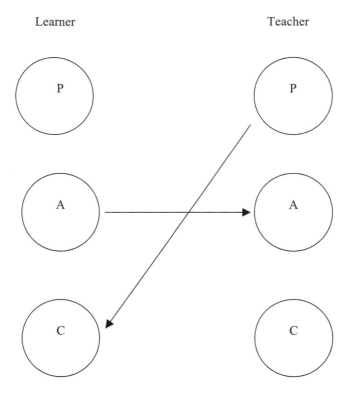

Figure 13.2 Crossed transactions

Bullies achieve satisfaction through dominating other people. They tend to target those who are sensitive and quiet, or with low self-esteem.

Bullies deliberately set out to hurt or damage their victim. Obvious forms of bullying include:

- hitting
- threatening physical violence

- being verbally aggressive
- invasion of personal space
- being humiliated
- racist taunts or gestures or graffiti
- unwanted physical contact or sexually abusive comments
- homophobic taunts

Less obvious forms include:

- excluding a learner from social groups
- teasing that goes too far
- spreading rumours
- hiding personal possessions

Incidents of bullying should be reported, and recorded, if serious. Bullying behaviour or threats of bullying should be investigated and in certain cases reported to the Police. Attempts should be made to stop the bullying, but if the bullying continues then the bully should be suspended or excluded.

Developing interpersonal and intrapersonal intelligences

In Chapter 4, 'What's the point of theory?', interpersonal intelligence and intrapersonal intelligence were described as two of a range of intelligences, which, if developed, help one resolve problems and manage difficulties. Learners with problem behaviour often need a lot of support to develop self-understanding and, in particular, an understanding of their emotions and motivation (intrapersonal intelligence). They also need support to develop an understanding of others, so that they can interact in a positive way with others, and establish relationships and maintain them (interpersonal intelligence). The lack of these two intelligences is, I believe, at the heart of the difficulties individuals often experience in their personal and work lives. One can have a satisfying life without being a maths wizard or being able to sing in tune, but if one lacks self-awareness and cannot get on comfortably with others, then life can be very hard-going.

Activity

Is the teacher using Critical Parent, Nurturing Parent or Adult tape in the following?

1   You have made a lot of silly mistakes. You have clearly rushed this work.
2   We expect you to give in your assignments on time, and for our part we will return them within seven days with written feedback.
3   If you are worried about anything at all, come and talk to me.

Is the learner using Adult or Child (Manipulative, Rebellious) tape?

4   You will pass me, won't you, so I don't have to do it all again.
5   Wow! I can't wait to get started!
6   You won't get me doing role play. I can't see the point.
7   Would you run over that function again for me?

Are the following transactions Reciprocal Transactions or Crossed Transactions?

8   Teacher: How do you feel you are doing on the course?
     Learner: I can understand what you say in French but I'm struggling with the grammar.
9   Learner: Sorry I was late – there was an accident on the way here.
     Teacher: You should leave home in time to allow for hold-ups.
10   Teacher: I notice you haven't given in your assignment yet.
     Learner: Lots of people haven't given in their assignments. Why pick on me?

(Answers to the questions are listed at the end of the chapter.)

Reflection

- Do you tend to use your Critical Parent tape or your Nurturing Parent tape more often?
- When did you last use your Rebellious or Manipulative Adaptive Child tape?
- How often do you respond with your Free Child tape, the one that is creative, fun-loving, and spontaneous?

Professional standards

This chapter relates to:

- Domain A: Professional values and practice
  AS3: Equality, diversity and inclusion in relation to learners, the workforce and the community
  AS7: Improving the quality of their practice.
- Domain B: Learning and teaching
  BS1: Maintaining an inclusive, equitable and motivating learning environment
  BS3: Communicating effectively and appropriately with learners to enhance learning.
- Domain D: Planning for learning
  DS1: Planning to promote equality, support diversity and to meet the aims and learning needs of learners

Further reading

Berne, E. (1996) *Games People Play*. New York: Random House.

Harris, T.A. (1995) *I'm OK – You're OK*. London: Arrow Books.

Rogers, B. (1997) *You Know the Fair Rule,* 2nd edn. London: Financial Times/ Prentice-Hall.

Rogers, B. (2006) *Classroom Behaviour*, 2nd edn. London: Paul Chapman.

Wallace, S. (2007a) *Getting the Buggers Motivated in FE*. London: Continuum International Group.

Stewart, I. and Joines,V. (1987) *TA Today – A New Introduction to Transactional Analysis*. Melton Mowbray: Lifespace Publishers.

Wallace, S. (2007b) *Managing Behaviour in the Lifelong Learning Sector*, 2nd edn. Exeter: Learning Matters.

Answers to the Activity

(1) Critical Parent; (2) Adult; (3) Nurturing Parent; (4) Manipulative Child (5) Free Child; (6) Rebellious Child; (7) Adult; (8) Reciprocal transaction – Adult to Adult/ Adult to Adult; (9) Crossed transaction – Adult to Adult/Critical Parent to Child; (10) Crossed transaction – Adult to Adult/Rebellious Child to Parent.

14   Disability barriers

Something to think about: The disabled learner is likely to know better than anyone else what help they may need.

What this chapter is about

- Approaches to disability
- Stereotypes, prejudice, and stigma
- Colours
- Resources and ICT
- Quiet spaces and change of venue

Approaches to disability

This chapter does not divide learners into 'normal' learners and 'disabled' learners. It is important to remember that every learner is a unique human being with talents. They may also have a disability, or more than one disability. You may be hard of hearing in one ear, I may get hay fever in the summer, he may have chronic back pains, but we do not define ourselves by these conditions. And neither should teachers refer to their learners as 'the hard-of-hearing learner' and so on.

Disabilities can act as barriers to learning. Teachers and learners should work together to discuss what helps and what hinders their learning. Each learner needs to be assessed individually and not under a blanket label as 'deaf' or 'wheelchair user'. Assumptions should not be made about someone's level of disability based on a previous experience of a person with the same disability. One deaf person may be a skilled lip-reader, another may have a signer with them, another may be partially deaf and able to hear in quiet environments.

It is also sensible to assume you have learners in your group who have not disclosed that they have a disability. This might be because:

- they feel ashamed;
- they fear rejection;
- they fear they will be made fun of;
- they may connect the word 'disability' with mobility and not with whatever disability they have.

Disabilities may be:

- physical disabilities
- learning difficulties
- mental health problems

The legal definition of disability is a physical or mental impairment that has a substantial, long-term adverse effect on a person's ability to carry out normal day-to-day activities. However, in the classroom, there are minor problems that fall just under the legal definition, but which are creating barriers to learning for the learner. A learner may be hard of hearing but not enough to be registered disabled. This emphasizes the importance of considering learners' needs on an individual basis.

The range of disabilities is wide and includes:

- hearing problems
- sight problems
- mobility problems
- facial disfigurement
- terminal or long-term illness
- eating disorders
- mental health problems, including depression and anxiety

Other, more specific disabilities include:

- *Dyslexia:* difficulties with oral and written language. Sometimes also difficulty with organizing, concentration or short-term memory.
- *Attention deficit hyperactivity d*isorder (ADHD): difficulty with concentration; heightened activity and impulsiveness.
- *Dysgraphia*: difficulties with handwriting.
- *Asperger syndrome*: difficulties with social communication, poor at reading visual 'cues', finds change unsettling, can be fixed on one interest to the exclusion of everything else, often above-average intelligence.

The disabled learner may need extra help from a support worker, or special equipment, or a different way of teaching. For example, a visually impaired learner wanted to do the first stage of a teaching qualification. As a team we decided it would be best if I gave him one-to-one tuition, as so much of the 'normal' sessions were visual, using handouts, the whiteboard, video and questionnaires, and case studies.

This occurred some time ago, and looking back I can see we were well- meaning, but the learner lost out on the benefits of taking part in discussions with the rest of the group. His understanding and insight into teaching would have been so much richer if he had been allowed to join the group.

I believe it is better for *everyone* if teachers incorporate as much choice as possible for *all* learners, not give only the disabled learner an alternative way of doing things. For example, learners can all be offered a choice of how to present their assignments. And the learning experience is enriched for everyone if teachers plan sessions to embrace learning styles that meet all needs.

Stereotypes, prejudice, and stigmas

A stigma involves the use of negative labels and being thought of as socially unacceptable. Negative labels include 'weirdo', 'bonkers', 'freak', 'a burden on society', 'pitiable', 'noble', 'stupid', 'thick', and 'victim'. Stigmas arise because of ignorance about the particular disability. Teachers need to update their knowledge and understanding about disabilities among their learners to be able to support them effectively. When people are prejudiced about a disability, they may react with fear or anxiety or avoid the disabled person. Disabled individuals often stigmatize themselves. They expect rejection and discrimination and so they withdraw.

People with mental health problems often meet with prejudice. Many experience a level of anxiety or depression that interferes with everyday life. Trying to get back to everyday life by mixing with other people, becoming a learner, getting and keeping a job, is made that much more of a struggle if they are treated with suspicion by others.

Feeling safe, having people in whom one can confide, feeling heard, and access to social networks all contribute to mental health. People need to feel a sense of worth, a sense of belonging, that they have some autonomy, and that they are being treated fairly. Poor living conditions, redundancy, social isolation, sensory or physical impairment, emotional or physical abuse, all can contribute to mental health problems.

Teachers can support learners who have mental health problems, or who have had them, by giving plenty of feedback and guidance, providing quiet places to work if they find it hard to concentrate, and by asking another learner to 'buddy up' (give support) with them, and give them support. Teachers should bear in mind that the learners will have 'good' days and 'bad' days.

Learners may miss sessions through illness, and may need the deadline extended for assignments to be handed in. Notes from missed sessions can be forwarded electronically to the learner at their home. At the same time, any negative comments from the rest of the group should be challenged, and strategies taken to increase the learner's sense of belonging.

Learners with epilepsy also experience prejudice, again through ignorance and fear. It can be frightening to watch someone have an epileptic episode. And sometimes they are discriminated against when they seek work, although there is no reason to turn down someone who has epilepsy unless there are health and safety concerns, such as when in charge of machinery. Because some learners do not reveal that they have epilepsy, I usually ask any new group to let me know privately, and explain that if I know, then I can take the right course of action if they have an episode.

Appearance is an extremely sensitive subject. Obesity can create barriers to learning, but it can also be greeted with a lack of sympathy or tolerance. In addition, learners who are obese may find they are excluded by the rest of the group.

We communicate looking into the faces of others. If the other person has a disfiguring birthmark or a disfigurement from an accident or surgery, then it can be difficult to look at them without feeling uncomfortable or maybe even revulsion. Although one may feel deep compassion, the person with the disfigurement most appreciates being treated and spoken to like anybody else. It takes away a person's dignity to be pitied. This applies to all disabilities.

Colours

Colour blindness affects almost as many of the population as dyslexia. It occurs mostly in males. It is recognized as a disability, yet I have never known anyone mention colour blindness on an enrolment form. The most common form of colour blindness is an inability to see red and green. If a learner driver comes across a man in the road holding up a flag, they have no idea if the flag is indicating 'green/go' or 'red/stop'. Attaching jump leads to a car or rewiring a plug involves identifying colours. Instructions on the television to 'press the red button' are of no use. Key words highlighted on the whiteboard with a green marker pen are missed. Many textbooks use colours to separate out passages or words.

Computers are awash with colours. Too often the background colour is in a shade of red with white writing that a person with colour blindness would not see. Anyone with colour blindness attending a programme on 'Computers for the Terrified' is going to be confused and frustrated. For experienced computer users, however, some websites have the facility for changing the colours.

It is easier to read information where there is a high contrast between the background and the foreground. Low-level light also has an adverse effect. If there is someone with colour blindness in a group, then it would make sense to ask them to complete a form evaluating how accessible they have found the information presented on the whiteboard, on the computer, on handouts and worksheets, and in textbooks. You could also ask yourself if you have given any instructions using the name of a colour without any other *clues* to what you are talking about. For example, it is helpful to say: 'Press the green button that says "next"', instead of 'Press the green button'.

Resources and ICT

Learners with dyslexia have difficulty with their reading, writing, and short-term memory. They may also need support with study skills, organizational skills, and time management. On the positive side, they often have good long-term memories, are creative thinkers, good at problem solving, and can provide fresh insights. They benefit from the following, which should be on a teacher's session plan anyway:

- an overview at the start of the session, giving the 'whole picture' before presenting the different parts;
- the main points should be emphasized, giving concrete examples so that the learner can build up a 'picture' of abstract ideas;
- handouts to refer to for consolidation and revision;
- visual, auditory, written, and hands-on activities;
- a summary at the end of the session.

In addition, dyslexic learners should be allowed to tape sessions if they wish to. Taking notes at the same time as listening to the teacher is difficult for them.

When teachers are aware of a learner's disability, they will take steps to ensure learners are still being included. For example, if a learner has a hearing impairment, the teacher should check that before they speak the learner is looking at them and can see their mouth, and when others ask questions, the teacher repeats the question. Similarly, with dyslexic learners, a teacher will build in regular pauses so that the learner has time to catch up with writing or reading.

Handouts are easier for dyslexic learners if they are in sans serif fonts such as Arial and on coloured paper with not too much text. When teachers write on the whiteboard they need to remember that lower-case letters, even for headings, are easier to read than capital letters. 'ELEPHANT' is a rectangular block, while 'elephant' is recognizable by the three upward sticks and the one downward stick.

There are many advantages for the dyslexic learner if they can use a computer for their work. They can use a spell check and a grammar check, and they will find using a keyboard less demanding than the physical act of writing. They can also change the screen colour, font style and size, and the line spacing to whatever suits them best. And where appropriate, learners should be able to present their work using camcorders, digital cameras or recorders.

Quiet spaces and change of venue

Some learners cannot cope with too much arousal. Being among a group of lively, motivated peers for sustained periods can affect them adversely. Learners with mental health problems may need to work quietly on their own from time to time. Some learners with medical conditions may tire easily and want regular breaks away from the main group. Learners with Asperger syndrome need routine without too much change. They will want to work quietly on their own at times.

Learners with ADHD can become challenging if they have to concentrate too long. A change of room, from classroom to computer room, meets their need for a new stimulus. This requires flexibility on the part of the teacher but it is better than allowing the learner to start disrupting the whole group. An added benefit is that learners with ADHD often seek attention and will set out to entertain the rest of the group. If they are working in a separate area, but within the sight of the teacher, then there is less opportunity for playing to the crowd.

Activity

1   What room layout would be best if you had a learner who was hard of hearing?
2   If a learner had severe arthritis in their hands, what problems might they experience on your programme?
3   How easy would it be for someone in a wheelchair or on crutches to join the rest of the group for a break of 15 minutes?

Reflection

Are some disabilities more acceptable to society than others?

Professional standards

This chapter relates to:

- Domain A: Professional values and practice
  AS 3: Equality, diversity and inclusion in relation to learners, the workforce and the community
- Domain B: Learning and teaching
  BS1: Maintaining an inclusive, equitable and motivating learning environment
  BS3: Communicating effectively and appropriately with learners to enhance learning
- Domain D: Planning for learning
  DS1: Planning to promote equality, support diversity and to meet the aims and learning needs of learners
  DS2: Learner participation in the planning of learning
- Domain E: Assessment for learning
  ES3: Learner involvement and shared responsibility in the assessment process

Further reading and useful websites

Braun, E.M. and Davis, R.D. (1997) *The Gift of Dyslexia, 2nd revised edn.* London: Souvenir Press.
Clarke, A. and Hesse, C. (2006) *Online Resources in the Classroom.* Leicester: NIACE.
Hardcastle, P. (2004) *Digital Cameras in Teaching and Learning.* Leicester: NIACE.

www.iamdyslexia.com
www.nas.org.uk
www.open.ac.uk/inclusiveteaching
www.techdis.ac.uk

15 Cultural awareness

Something to think about: Can one culture ever fully understand the reality of another culture?

What this chapter is about

- What is culture?
- Culture and human rights
- Cultural values
- Religion and belief
- Working within the community
- Young learners who slip through the net
- Lifelong learning and the elderly

What is culture?

Culture is a system of behaviours and beliefs that are shared by a group and passed down from one generation to the next. By providing a blueprint of what is acceptable, the people within the group are able to live together more or less harmoniously, and they have a set of guidelines for their actions. However, culture evolves, with succeeding generations. External influences encourage acceptance of new ways of doing things. The 'old guard' often fiercely resists change. This can create conflict between the younger and older members of a culture. There is usually a dominant culture, and often other cultures, or sub-cultures, are compared unfavourably.

In a world where many cultures live side by side, it is important to work towards an understanding of each others' beliefs and customs, and to communicate with each other in ways that foster trust and respect. Where there are negative attitudes towards other cultures – suspicion, avoidance, fear, rejection – teachers can start by first reflecting on their own attitudes to other cultures, and then finding positive ways to explore similarities and differences between cultures with their learners.

We can become emotional and judgemental about child-rearing practices, food (junk food, fresh organic food), modesty (from showing too much to completely covering up), and attitudes to work and state benefits.

A learner's culture must be accepted as part of the learner. A teacher can only be fully supportive when they can put themselves in the shoes of the learner and see life from their perspective.

For example, a group of immigrants wanted to find work and first needed some training. However, the teaching team recognized that these potential learners did not come from a culture that lived by the clock. (And when you think about it, many people are now slaves to time-keeping.) Punctuality was not a concept that was necessary in their former lives. Clearly, they would not get the full benefits of their learning if they turned up to class half an hour after the start, or if they attended irregularly. A pre-training programme was therefore designed to induct them into the requirements of being a learner. The certificate they gained also included criteria relating to attendance and punctuality.

Culture and human rights

We all see life differently. The diversity of different cultures, and their different ways of life and beliefs, creates an interesting society. All groups should be treated fairly and with dignity, and opportunities given for them to reach their full potential. All groups have a right to:

- live the life they choose;
- protection from discrimination;
- education;
- freedom of expression;
- freedom of thought, belief, and religion.

Cultural values

It helps to understand that some cultures are based on individualism and some are based on collectivism. Cultures based on individualism:

- are flexible about the roles within the family;
- have relationships where everyone is equal;
- promote independence and self-expression;
- focus on the potential of the individual.

Cultures based on collectivism:

- have stable, hierarchical roles;
- respect authority and elders;
- are interdependent;
- hold the family and the community as more important than the individual, who is socialized to put their own needs secondary to those of the family.

Someone from a culture based on individualism has a sense of personal responsibility and when they transgress, they experience guilt at a personal level. In a culture which is based on collectivism, shame and humiliation is felt by the whole group when one of their members transgresses. An individual's behaviour impacts on the whole community.

Where a man is part of a patriarchal society, he will not feel comfortable discussing problems with teachers or help agencies, particularly dealing with a woman. It would be considered losing face, and he would feel humiliated.

Attitudes to appearance can be misunderstood by the two types of culture. One attitude is that it shows high self-esteem to make the most of one's appearance and look as physically attractive as possible. When others cover up, it is interpreted that they have low self-esteem. In fact, in a collectivist culture, it is undignified to publicly display one's attractiveness. This is a private matter, for within the family at home.

The concept of everyone being equal is alien to someone from a hierarchal community. For example, a Hindu learner was on an interpersonal skills programme, and the teacher was explaining the 'I'm OK – You're OK' model described in Chapter 13. The learner did not accept that her sister-in-law was equal to herself. Because the learner's husband was the older brother and therefore had responsibility towards his younger brother, it was right, she maintained, that the brother-in-law and sister-in-law should defer to her and her husband. Beliefs such as these are deeply engrained, and where the teacher has different beliefs, they need to reflect on respecting the cultural beliefs of another. At the same time, they need to bear in mind the principles of human rights.

Some cultures are socialized not to say 'no' to elders and parents. It is disrespectful. They may also not say what they mean, but say what will please others. Many women lower their eyes and their heads when speaking to a male or an older female. This can be misinterpreted by westerners in an interview or work situation. It comes across as lacking in confidence and assertiveness. Teachers need to imagine how difficult it must be for a woman to change and make eye contact, behaving in what must seem, to them, a brazen way.

It can be equally difficult the other way around, when a western woman is expected to adapt her body language. A Kurd, married to an English woman, was distressed that his wife smiled and talked to other men, making eye contact. For the wife, it would have meant a change of personality to behave in a submissive way in front of a man. Similarly, a woman accustomed to being submissive may feel changing the way she interacts is too great a step to take. On the other hand, she may decide to compromise and to behave one way at work and another at home.

The assumption that to lead a satisfying life one needs to develop one's full potential as an individual, is not shared by all cultures, and the teacher needs to bear this in mind.

Religion and belief

A religion involves:

- belief in a supreme being;

- worship of that supreme being;
- a group of people who all observe customs, values, and beliefs that have been set down by the supreme being.

This would include the main religions of Christianity, Islam, Buddhism, Judaism, Hinduism, Sikhism, and Rastafarianism.

Under human rights law, Humanism is defined as a *belief*. Its philosophy is that we can lead a good life based on humanity and reason without the need for religious beliefs. As well as the right to hold one's own religious or philosophical beliefs, everyone has a right to have no religion or belief.

Therefore, learners should be supported in their religious beliefs, and should not be pressurized into changing their beliefs, but they should not be discriminated against if they do change their beliefs. Similarly, no-one should be discriminated against because they have no religion or belief. Someone who practises a religion is not superior to someone who has no religion, and vice versa.

Teachers should be informed enough about the religion of any of their learners to respond sensitively to any needs relating to:

- *Prayer*: for example, a Muslim who prays at set times during the day. They will need a private room to go to. Women will need a separate room from men.
- *Fasting*: several religions have periods in the year when they fast and may find concentration hard. It may be fairer to re-schedule assessment dates.
- *Food*: certain foods or ways of preparing them are prohibited in some religions. Therefore, thought should be given to choice of food when bringing food into the classroom, or going out on visits.

Working within the community

There are hard-to-reach groups who have become socially excluded and who are unlikely to be found on mainstream programmes in colleges or adult centres. I visited one community where the hopelessness of the people in that road was apparent from the piles of junk in every front garden, the broken toys, the graffiti and the rundown appearance of every dwelling. The community was made up of the elderly, single parents, and people with learning difficulties. None of them was in employment. The church premises in the road was used as a community centre, which was within easy distance for everyone, and which felt more welcoming and less intimidating than a larger organization.

Teachers and volunteers looked at ways to develop the potential of the adults in the community and to give them back their self-respect. One idea was to give them the skills to improve their community and to help each other. The programme, 'Community Work Skills', was regularly over-subscribed because neighbours told each other about it. The programme provided an understanding of:

- how community groups work towards shared community work objectives;

- what community work seeks out to achieve;
- the general values that are central to community work;
- the role of community workers;
- how disempowerment affects individuals and communities;
- co-operative practice within a group work situation.

The programme showed learners how the members of a community could take some control over their lives and take actions to improve their circumstances. Importantly, it encouraged them to support each other. One ex-learner worked in a voluntary capacity, phoning and visiting new learners to maintain their motivation, creating networks, and writing a monthly newsletter. Another learner in her eighties, with hearing problems, went on to serve refreshments at the community centre. An ex-drug addict became a parish councillor. Both of them were actively contributing to their community and felt that what they were doing was worthwhile. Other learners went on to further learning opportunities at the centre. This is an example of giving fresh impetus to a whole community where lack of employment, finance, and opportunity have given them little hope of a better future.

A sexual health advisory organization recruited teenage mothers to a pro-gramme that not only increased their knowledge of sexual health issues, but gave them the skills to pass on their knowledge to other teenage girls. This benefited the mothers, easing them back into learning and giving them a qualification. Also, the teenage girls responded better when their facilitators were young women who had become pregnant, rather than hearing about sexual health from, for example, middle aged, middle-class women.

Some schemes in the community are aimed at involving fathers, particularly non-resident fathers, more with their children. There is no formal learning pro-gramme. The community centre sets up activities and events that are designed to give fathers the experience and opportunity to interact with their children. Parent and child coffee mornings are not likely to appeal, but fathers would probably welcome a day out flying kites, a trip on a canal boat or playing football in the park.

While the community centre may feel a welcoming place to local mothers, where the social workers are more often than not women, fathers may find the environment uninviting. At one centre, a community worker decided to look at the centre as if she were a father. She noticed that as soon as she stepped through the door she was faced with a poster relating to domestic violence, and there was a further poster on rape. The impression was that men were viewed very negatively.

Young learners who slip through the net

Young people who have been in prison, are on probation, are in sheltered accommo-dation or of no fixed abode, or may have been in care, often slip through the net and are not in education, employment or training. These are young people who have:

- low educational achievement
- literacy problems

- English as a second language
- learning or behavioural difficulties

They will not respond well to traditional learning environments or traditional learning methods. Any assessment with written work will put them off if they have learning difficulties or have issues with confidence.

They will feel more comfortable in an environment more like a youth centre. The programmes need to have a youth culture focus, and through that, develop the skills that they need:

- *Life skills*: working as a team, communicating effectively.
- *Skills to enhance employability*: writing CVs, interview skills.
- *Personal development*: confidence, assertiveness.

Through outdoor activities, and projects that are practical and creative like film making, art, and music, the skills of co-operation, planning, and seeing a project through to completion can be developed.

Programmes for hard-to-reach groups such as these will mean a larger staff to learner ratio than usual, and staff need to be drawn from a wide range of sources. The staff selected should have an empathy with the young people and should have an ability to communicate with them and a belief that they are worthwhile human beings, because society has more or less washed their hands of them. When programmes such as these work, the young people learn the pleasure of making friends and working productively with them, their confidence increases, and their attitude to learning changes.

Some teachers give written feedback on each young person's learning journey, based on the personal goals they have identified at the start of the programme. For example, if the learner has said they want to work on building up their confidence to communicate their ideas to others, then the teacher will give feedback on the first day, midway through the programme, and at the end of the programme.

The comments will give plenty of encouragement but also be clear about the challenges facing the learner. The initial comment might be along the lines of: 'Well done, for being so positive about the programme. It's clear you have lots of interesting ideas, and we would like to hear more of them. I know it is scary sometimes to speak out in front of others, but your challenge is to overcome this by the end of the programme'. The mid-programme feedback might be: 'You gave good, sound reasons why you preferred one project rather than another. This really helped the group make a final decision. When another learner was stuck, you gave him suggestions'. The end-of-programme feedback might be: 'You have accomplished your personal learning goal – well done! The presentation you gave to the group showed that you can now express yourself with confidence'.

Lifelong learning and the elderly

Mainstream's attitude to the elderly influences the access the elderly have to learning. China has extensive provision of learning for the elderly. Programmes range from philosophy, flower growing, and calligraphy to how to care for the sick, herbal medicine, and exercise. Other cultures are not so forward thinking.

Elderly people sometimes feel they are too old to learn or are inhibited by the cost of programmes or their lack of mobility. Keeping one's mind active, mixing socially, and feeling useful all add to mental health. The elderly can feel they have outlived their usefulness and are forgotten by society because they are no longer in work.

The University of the Third Age (U3A) is a self-help, self-managed, lifelong learning cooperative for older people who are no longer in full-time work, providing opportunities to share learning experiences in a wide range of interests and to pursue learning not for qualifications, but for fun. Older learners are also attracted to programmes that give them the skills to work as volunteers in the community. Many older learners, the 'silver surfers', are computer literate, and programmes that they can access on-line may be their only option if they are housebound.

There is a Chinese proverb: 'At dusk, do not say it is too late, do say that there is sunshine all over the sky'. Older learners are a neglected sector of the community.

Activity

Organizations have cultures of their own. Evaluate the culture of your own organization by looking at the following statements and questions.

1   What cultural groups are represented among senior management, teachers, learners, and administration?
2   The organization is working towards an understanding of different cultural values.
3   Different community groups are included in training events.
4   Records are kept of different languages spoken by staff and learners.
5   Holy days from different religions are recognized appropriately.
6   Cultural differences are respected by all cultures involved.

Reflection

- How difficult would you find it to adapt to a different culture?
- How might you be different from the way you are if you were part of another culture?

Professional standards

This chapter relates to:

- Domain A: Professional values and practice

AS2: Learning, its potential to benefit people emotionally, intellectually, socially and economically, and its contribution to community sustainability
AS3: Equality, diversity and inclusion in relation to learners, the workforce and the community
AS5: Collaboration with other individuals, groups and/or organizations with a legitimate interest in the progress and development of learners
- Domain C: Specialist learning and teaching
  CS1: Understanding and keeping up to date with current knowledge in respect of own specialist area
- Domain D: Planning for learning
  DS1: Planning to promote equality, support diversity and to meet the aims and learning needs of learners
- Domain E: Assessment for learning
  ES2: Assessing the work of learners in a fair and equitable manner
- Domain F: Access and progression
  FS3: Maintaining own professional knowledge in order to provide information on opportunities for progression in own specialist area
  FS4: A multi-agency approach to supporting development and progression opportunities for learners

Further reading and useful websites

Aldridge, F. and Tuckett, A. (2007) *What Older People Learn*. Leicester: NIACE.
Clarke, A. (2006) *Teaching Adults ITC Skills*. Exeter: Learning Matters.
Thompson, J. (2002) *Community Education and Neighbourhood Renewal*. Leicester: NIACE.

www.u3a.org.uk

Appendices

Appendix 1   Continuing Professional Development (CPD)

Teachers do not stop developing professionally once they have their initial qualifications. They need to keep up-to-date with their subject specialism, emerging technologies, changes in national standards, and changes made by awarding bodies. They also need to refresh their teaching and learning approaches. Teachers on programmes funded by government bodies are required to provide evidence of their CPD every year in order to continue to be licensed teachers.

Full-time teachers should log a minimum of 30 hours CPD a year. Part-time teachers would be expected to log 15 hours if they have a half time post. A minimum of six hours is required even if a teacher is only teaching for an hour a week. Reflection on CPD is central to the process. Teachers should not only log what activities they have undertaken, but keep a reflective account of the impact the activities have had on their professional practice and on their learners.

Decisions about what CPD to engage in are usually based on feedback from learners, appraisals, being observed while teaching, the training organization's development plan, and changes in the teaching world. Teachers can then draw up an individual development plan to include the activities, the objectives for each activity, the action plan and time-scale, and a column for recording what was achieved and what the outcomes were for the teacher and the learners.

Continuing professional development can cover a wide range of activities, not only attending subject specialism conferences, workshops, and formal qualifications. It might also be designing new curricula, delivering staff development activities, mentoring new colleagues, team teaching, secondments, writing articles, membership of steering groups or reviewing books.

Appendix 2   QTLS Standards – Domain B

The professional standards for teachers, tutors, and trainers in the lifelong learning sector are divided into six domains: professional values and practice, learning and teaching, specialist learning and teaching, planning for learning, assessment for learning, access and progression.

Each Domain consists of professional values, professional knowledge and understanding, and professional practice. Domain B, learning and teaching, is given here as an example. You may want to assess yourself against the standards. You can first check that you agree with the values, and then check if, after reading 'Supporting Learners in the Lifelong Learning Sector', you now have the knowledge and understanding. Finally, if you are a practising teacher, you can assess yourself against the standards for professional practice.

Professional values

Teachers in the lifelong learning sector value:

- AS1: Learners, their progress and development, their learning goals and aspirations and the experience they bring to their learning
- AS2: Learning, its potential to benefit people emotionally, intellectually, socially and economically, and its contribution to community sustainability
- AS3: Equality, diversity and inclusion in relation to learners, the workforce and the community
- AS4: Reflection and evaluation of their own practice and their continuing professional development as teachers
- AS5: Collaboration with other individuals, groups and/or organizations with a legitimate interest in the progress and development of learners.

Teachers are committed to:

- BS1: Maintaining an inclusive, equitable and motivating learning environment
- BS2: Applying and developing own professional skills to enable learners to achieve their goals
- BS3: Communicating effectively and appropriately with learners to enhance learning

- BS4: Collaboration with colleagues to support the needs of learners
- BS5: Using a range of learning resources to support learners

Professional knowledge and understanding

Teachers know and understand:

- BK1.1: Ways to maintain a learning environment in which learners feel safe and supported
- BK1.2: Ways to develop and manage behaviours which promote respect for and between others and create an equitable and inclusive learning environment
- BK1.3: Ways of creating a motivating learning environment
- BK2.1: Principles of learning and ways to provide learning activities to meet curriculum requirements and the needs of learners
- BK2.2: Ways to engage, motivate and encourage active participation of learners and learner independence
- BK2.3: The relevance of learning approaches, preferences and skills to learner progress
- BK2.4: Flexible delivery of learning, including open and distance learning and on-line learning
- BK2.5: Ways of using learners' own experiences as a foundation for learning
- BK2.6: Ways to evaluate own practice in terms of efficiency and effectiveness
- BK2.7: Ways in which mentoring and/or coaching can support the development of professional skills and knowledge
- BK3.1: Effective and appropriate use of different forms of communication informed by relevant theories and principles
- BK3.2: A range of listening and questioning techniques to support learning
- BK3.3: Ways to structure and present information and ideas clearly and effectively to learners
- BK3.4: Barriers and aids to effective communication
- BK3.5: Systems for communication within own organization
- BK4.1: Good practice in meeting the needs of learners in collaboration with colleagues
- BK5.1: The impact of resources on effective learning
- BK5.2: Ways to ensure that resources used are inclusive, promote equality and support diversity.

Professional practice

Teachers:

- BP1.1: Establish a purposeful learning environment where learners feel safe, secure, confident and valued

- BP1.2: Establish and maintain procedures with learners which promote and maintain appropriate behaviour, communication and respect for others, while challenging discriminatory behaviour and attitudes
- PB1.3: Create a motivating environment which encourages learners to reflect on, evaluate and make decisions about their learning
- BP2.1: Provide learning activities which meet curriculum requirements and the needs of all learners
- BP2.2: Use a range of effective and appropriate teaching and learning techniques to engage and motivate learners and encourage independence
- BP2.3: Implement learning activities which develop the skills and approaches of all learners and promote learner autonomy
- BP2.4: Apply flexible and varied delivery methods as appropriate to teaching and learning practice
- BP2.5: Encourage learners to use their own life experiences as a foundation for their development
- BP2.6: Evaluate the efficiency and effectiveness of own teaching including consideration of learner feedback and learning theories
- BP2.7: Use mentoring and/or coaching to support own and others' professional development, as appropriate
- BP3.1: Communicate effectively and appropriately using different forms of language and media, including written, oral and non-verbal communication, and new and emerging technologies to enhance learning
- BP3.2: Use listening and questioning techniques appropriately and effectively in a range of learning contexts
- BP3.3: Structure and present information clearly and effectively
- BP3.4: Evaluate and improve own communication skills to maximize effective communication and overcome identifiable communication barriers
- BP3.5: Identify and use appropriate organizational systems for communicating with learners and colleagues
- BP4.1: Collaborate with colleagues to encourage learner progress
- BP5.1: Select and develop a range of effective resources, including appropriate use of new and emerging technologies
- BP5.2: Select, develop and evaluate resources to ensure they are inclusive, promote equality and engage with diversity

Appendix 3   Icebreakers

Icebreakers are useful for fostering trust and acceptance. Some teachers only use 'sensible' icebreakers, others feel comfortable with more frivolous ones. An icebreaker that makes learners laugh and relax can get a group to gel quickly. With groups that need warming up every session, a quick icebreaker can put them in the mood for learning.

The following are just a selection from the huge number of ideas that can be found on the internet.

1   *Non-verbal interviews.* Put learners in pairs. One person provides information about themselves without speaking. They may draw or point; for instance, they could point to a wedding ring or draw a house. Their partner then tells the rest of the group what they think they have learned about the other person.

2   *Memory game.* The group sit in a circle. The first person says their name and one fact about themselves: 'I'm Angie and I have two cats'. The next person introduces not only themselves but the first person. 'I'm Joe and I play the guitar. This is Angie and she has two cats'. The third person introduces themselves and Joe and Angie.

3   *Finding out about a partner.* Each person is given a list of questions to ask a partner, such as:
    - Are you a morning person or a night owl?
    - What is your favourite food?
    - What food do you hate?
    - What would you like to be doing tomorrow?
    - What are your favourite TV programmes?
    - If you won the lottery tomorrow, what is the first thing you would buy?

4   *True or false?* The teacher holds up a card with three statements about themselves such as:
    (a)   I speak Chinese
    (b)   I ride a bicycle to work
    (c)   My hobby is train spotting

The learners are told that two statements are true and one is false. They are invited to say which statement they think is false, and why. They then write two true and one false statements about themselves. Depending on the number in the class, they can then guess which is the false statement in small groups or as part of the whole group.

5   *Scavenger Hunt.* Give learners ten minutes to collect all the items on a list from others in the group. They may only take one item per person. The items could be:

- A driving licence
- A photograph
- A pen
- A book
- A shop receipt
- A watch
- A scarf

6   *Give each learner a large piece of paper.* Ask them to write each letter of their name down the left-hand side. They then choose a word that starts with each letter. The word should describe the learner. Beside each word, the learner draws a picture that illustrates the description.

7   *Too Many Cooks.* Cut up a recipe, so that the title, the ingredients, and instructions are all separated. Groups try to put the recipe in the right order. The first to finish shouts out 'Bon appetit'. Instead of a recipe, it could be instructions for, say, withdrawing money from a cash machine.

8   *Balloon race.* Each learner ties a balloon round their ankle. Their task is to pop the balloon of everyone else. When someone's balloon is popped, they are no longer in the game.

Appendix 4 Memory – Visual Associations

Remembering is easier if one makes a visual association. This method is fun to do and it is surprising how often learners have 100 per cent recall the next day or following week.

The first step is to put the following list up for everyone to see. Note that 'one' rhymes with 'gun' and two rhymes with 'shoe', and so on.

1 Gun
2 Shoe
3 Tree
4 Door
5 Hive
6 Sticks
7 Heaven
8 Gate
9 Line
10 Hen

Then, the objects that the learners want to remember (maybe ingredients for a dish) are written beside each word, such as: onion, garlic cloves, butter, slice of bacon, mince, tin of tomatoes, mushrooms, ketchup, tube of tomato puree, pepper.

The learners visualize each object with the words in the list. For example, the onion could be visualized coming out of the barrel of the gun, and the garlic cloves forming a pattern on a shoe, and the butter hanging from a branch of the tree. When all the objects have been visualized, ask what was object number one, or what was associated with the gun. You will find that you can jump around and ask what object number nine was, then ask what was number five, and usually learners remember with ease.

Appendix 5   Referencing and Bibliographies

If an author is quoted or their words paraphrased in an assignment, it is acknowledged as follows, either within the sentence or at the end of the sentence:

> Mary Smith (2007, p. 12) wrote: 'Grammar schools compare favourably with private schools'.

> or

> 'Grammar schools have results equally as good as private schools' (Smith 2007, p. 12).

It is essential to include references to avoid plagiarism (claiming the theories/ideas are one's own) and out of courtesy to the authors.

At the end of the assignment, one should include a list of the details of all the references. A bibliography can include references but also other sources that have not been mentioned in the assignment. The list should be in alphabetical order (authors' surnames) and in the following sequence:

- Surname
- Initials
- Year of publication, in parentheses
- Title, in italics
- Town of publication
- Publisher

Berne, E. (1996) *Games People Play*. New York: Random House.

Maslow, A.H. (1998) *Towards a Psychology of Being*. New York: John Wiley.

Trower, P., Casey, A. and Dryden, W. (1998) *Cognitive Behavioural Counselling in Action*. London: Sage.

If articles from journals or magazines are being cited, the format is as follows:

- Surname
- Initials
- Year of publication, in parentheses
- Title of article
- Name of journal, in italics

- Volume number
- Page range

Website addresses are listed as follows:

- The website
- Author
- Year
- Title
- Date website was accessed

Appendix 6   Individual Learning Plans

Individual Learning Plans form the basis for learners, in discussion with teachers, to identify long- and short- term goals, to review and record progress and achievements, and to plan for future development. Such plans also help the teacher plan for differentiated teaching and learning activities.

INDIVIDUAL LEARNING PLAN
NAME OF LEARNER: NAME OF TEACHER:
PROGRAMME NAME: START DATE:
RESULTS OF ASSESSMENTS: (e.g. Learning Style Questionnaire, English/Maths/ICT)   (Using, for example, interview, test, self-assessment, discussion in groups)
RELEVANT QUALIFICATIONS/EXPERIENCE:
LEARNING SUPPORT NEEDS/ARRANGEMENTS
LONG-TERM GOAL:
PERSONAL/SOCIAL SHORT-TERM TARGETS
PROGRESS REVIEW 1:
PROGRESS REVIEW 2:
RECORD OF ACHIEVEMENT: ACHIEVEMENT OF PERSONAL TARGETS:
PLANS FOR PROGRESSION:

Appendix 7   Schemes of Work

The two schemes of work that follow are on the same topic, but there are differences in the ages, genders, needs, and interests of the two groups, and variations in the resources available. Therefore, the schemes have been adapted accordingly.

Scheme 1: is for a group of six teenage girls who are low achievers on an entry-into-employment programme. They respond best when activities are aimed at their interests. The current way they present themselves would put them at a disadvantage with potential employers.

AIM: To develop learners' presentation skills					
OUTCOME: By the end of the programme learners will have: ● Delivered a 4-minute presentation using two resources ● Identified own strengths and areas for improvement					
Week	Outcome	Resources	Teacher activity	Learner activity	Assessment
1	Plan chosen topic	Handout: How to plan a presentation	Briefing Question and answer Explanation (structuring a talk) Coaching Summarizing	Brainstorm themes and topics Answer questions Mindmapping Plan talks	Written plans
2	Identify characteristics of a good delivery	Object cards Opinion cards Observation checklists	Question and answer (Non-verbal communication) Briefing Feedback Briefing	Answer questions 1-minute talk on object on card Self-assessment	Completed observation checklists

				Feedback Demonstration of poor non-verbal communication	Answer questions 1-minute talk on opinion on subject on card Self-assessment Observe demonstra-tion Complete checklist	
3	Select and design visual aids	Examples of visual aids Computers Flipchart paper/pens Magazines	Present examples of visual aids Demonstrate Coach	Brainstorm visual aids Observe demonstra-tion Design visual aids	Completed visual aids	
4	Deliver and evaluate a presentation	Self-assessment forms	Recap on assessment procedure Observe/ feedback	Deliver presentation Reflect on strengths and areas for improvement	Observation of presentation Oral reflections	

Figure A1   Scheme of work for teenage girls

Scheme 2: is for a group of six men who will be making speeches at weddings. They are inexperienced and hide their self-consciousness behind humour, but they are keen to learn.

AIM: To give learners the knowledge and skills to deliver effective speeches					
OUTCOME: By the end of the programme learners will have: • Delivered an appropriate, structured wedding speech using prompt cards • Evaluated their delivery					
Week	Outcome	Resources	Teacher activity	Learner activity	Assessment
1	Identify characteristics of good and bad wedding speeches	Video of selected wedding speeches	Assess needs Question Play video Lead discussions	Identify own wedding role Recall good and bad speeches Observe video and evaluate deliveries Draw up criteria for a good speech Brainstorm purpose of speech for groom/ father/best man	Group's list of criteria
2	Demonstrate effective use of timing and non-verbal communication	Topic cards Handout: jokes for weddings	Brief first task Discuss deliveries Brief second task Discuss deliveries Discuss timing, eye contact, and non-verbal communication Feedback	Seated, talk for 1 minute on topic on card Standing, talk for 1 minute on topic on card Tell a joke Select joke from list Feedback	Observation of talks and jokes

3	Plan and deliver a 3-minute speech using prompt cards	Handout: planning a speech Prompt cards	Lead discussion Describe the three stage structure of a speech/use of prompt cards Coach/ feedback	Brainstorm the appropriate content for different roles Mindmap own speech Prepare prompt cards Deliver speech	
4	Evaluate own delivery	Camcorder Camera operator Monitor	Observe Feedback	Deliver speech to camera Watch playback Identify strengths/ weaknesses	Oral self-evaluation of recorded speech

Figure A2   Scheme of work for adult males

Appendix 8   Aims and Objectives

The teacher has aims, the learner achieves objectives. Aims are expressed in general terms, objectives are more specific. The following examples may help you when you are writing your own aims and objectives.

Examples of teachers' aims:

- To give practice in oral fluency
- To develop co-ordination skills
- To give learners the opportunity to experiment with colour
- To foster positive tolerance
- To raise awareness of the role of accounting in society
- To enable learners to explore the diverse range of ancient world studies
- To prepare learners for job interviews
- To develop a sense of responsibility
- To give the understanding, skills, and confidence to enjoy mountain skiing
- To give learners the language skills needed on holiday

There is a saying, 'If you don't know where you're going, any bus will do'. In teaching, you need to know what new skill, knowledge, understanding or change of feeling/ attitude you want your learners to acquire, otherwise the structure of your session will have no focus.

Objectives should state very clearly what you want learners to be able to do by the end of the session. The verbs at the start of each objective below are specific in a way that enables a teacher to assess if the objectives have been achieved.

- Design an advert for your chosen product
- Carry out a questionnaire survey
- Produce an outline business plan
- Create a master slide for a Power Point presentation
- List some basic needs of a child
- Describe some ground rules and state why they are important
- Use appropriate phrases for interruption
- Respond to questions on familiar topics
- Give a short talk to a known group on a familiar topic
- Create, save, and print a spreadsheet
- Edit a document
- Take and record correct body measurements
- Cut pattern to individual's measurement and size

- Give two examples of good communication
- Organize two different icebreakers within the group
- Explain a range of rights/choices including why they are important
- Define diversity and equality opportunities and describe the relationship between them
- Participate in a group discussion
- Justify the choice of activities
- Evaluate own performance

Appendix 9 Right Brain/Left Brain Learning Style Questionnaire

Read the questions below and put a tick by your answer.

1 I remember people's faces
   (a) no
   (b) yes

2 If I had to assemble some flat pack furniture, I would
   (a) lay out all the parts and the tools and follow the directions
   (b) have a quick look at the directions and then use guesswork to put the parts together

3 I prefer
   (a) multiple-choice questions
   (b) essay-type assignments

4 If learning a dance routine, it is easier for me
   (a) if the teacher gives a verbal explanation and then I repeat the action in my head
   (b) if I can watch a demonstration and then practise

5 I prefer to be given jobs where
   (a) I can complete one task at a time
   (b) I multi-task, doing several tasks at the same time

6 I get more pleasure from
   (a) making improvements to something
   (b) creating something new

7 When I am concentrating on reading I like
   (a) silence
   (b) music in the background

8   I usually know what time it is without looking at my watch
     (a)   yes
     (b)   no

9   I like learning to be presented
     (a)   logically, with details and facts
     (b)   as an overview, looking at the whole picture

10 I organize my work and personal life and do not run over time
     (a)   yes
     (b)   no

11 I like my days
     (a)   to be planned so I know exactly what I will be doing
     (b)   to be fluid enough so that I can change my plans if I want to

12 If I have to make up my mind about an issue
     (a)   I weigh up all the facts
     (b)   I go with what my emotional instinct

Instructions: add up the number of ticks for answer (a) and add up the ticks for answer (b). To calculate your score, put a minus (–) sign in front of your total (a) score and a plus (+) sign in front of your total (b) score and work out the sum.

Example: –8 + 2 = –6

Scores:

–12 to –10 very strong left-brain dominance

–8 to –6 moderate left-brain dominance

–4 to –2 slight left-brain preference

0 no preference

+2 to +4 slight right-brain preference

+6 to +8 moderate right-brain dominance

+10 to +12 very strong right-brain dominance

Left-brain learners:

- have a good short-term memory
- think in words
- are time-conscious
- remember sequences
- like information to be presented step by step in logical sequence
- are good at analysis

Right-brain learners:

- are space-conscious
- think in images
- remember patterns
- like to see the whole picture
- make intuitive links
- remember by making personal associations

Appendix 10: Activist/Reflector/ Theorist/ Pragmatist Questionnaire

Honey and Mumford designed a lengthy questionnaire to determine preferred learning styles. The short questionnaire presented here does not pretend to be scientific, but it will show you which learning style you lean towards. Put a tick against each statement you agree with.

1   I don't like unstructured activities
2   I don't like activities where I have to talk about my feelings
3   I like to be shown an example that I can copy
4   I enjoy new experiences, problems, and opportunities
5   I like activities that have an immediate practical benefit
6   I like to stand back and listen to what others have to say
7   I like working in groups, role playing or problem solving
8   I don't like doing things without preparation
9   I like structured activities that have a clear purpose
10   I want to take action, not sit around talking
11   I like to think things through before making up my mind
12   I tend to take the role of leader when I'm in a group
13   I don't rush into making decisions
14   I like the excitement of being thrown into the deep end
15   I enjoy trying out new ideas with feedback from an expert
16   I like the opportunity to question and to probe

Scoring:

Activists will have ticked questions 4, 7, 12, 14

Reflectors will have ticked questions 6, 8, 11, 13

Theorists will have ticked questions 1, 2, 9, 16

Pragmatists will have ticked questions 3, 5, 10, 15

(You may have a strong preference for one learning style or a mixture of styles.)

Teachers who are Activists need to be careful they do not overload their sessions with lots of exciting activities. Learners also need the opportunity to reflect on what they have learned from the activity and how they can apply it.

Teachers who are Reflectors should check that their sessions do not consist of lots of discussions. Learners should also be encouraged to draw conclusions and to come up with suggested actions.

Teachers who are Theorists may spend most of their sessions lecturing, with the learners making notes. They need to ensure learners are also given activities connected with the lecture, time to reflect on what they have heard, and opportunities to discuss how they could use their new knowledge.

Teachers who are Pragmatists may throw learners in at the deep end, giving them problems to solve, without first giving them enough information and time to think through the options.

Appendix 11: VAK Learning Style Questionnaire

Find out if you are an Auditory, Visual or Kinaesthetic learner.

Read the following statements and tick the ones that apply to you.

- I learn by listening (A)
- I talk out loud to myself (A)
- I usually speak slowly (C)
- I usually speak quickly (B)
- I doodle when I'm talking to people (B)
- I express myself fluently (A)
- I am a good speller (B)
- I am easily distracted by noise (A)
- I am talkative and I enjoy discussions (A)
- I often forget instructions given verbally (B)
- I am good at planning and organizing (B)
- I touch people to get their attention (C)
- I find it difficult to sit still (C)
- My handwriting is messy (C)
- I forget to pass on messages (B)
- I am neat and tidy (B)
- I am better at explaining things verbally than putting them in writing (A)
- I often move my lips or say the words out loud as I am reading (A)
- When I am telling a story I act it out (C)
- I only remember where places are on a map if I have been there (C)

Add up the number of ticks for (A), (B), and (C) statements.

If you mostly ticked (A) statements you learn best by listening to others lecturing, discussing or giving verbal instructions. You find it hard to listen and take notes at the same time. If you ticked mostly (B) statements you learn best from diagrams, pictures, maps and other visual ways of presenting information. If you ticked mostly (C) statements you learn best through hands-on activities. However, some people have a mixture of learning styles.

Appendix 12: Study Skills

Assess your strengths and weaknesses. Look at each statement and put an 'A' for always, an 'S' for sometimes or an 'R' for rarely.

Organizing and planning

- I make a list of tasks
- I prioritize important and urgent tasks
- I spread the tasks for large assignments over several days
- I make a timetable and stick to it
- My notes and files are organized
- I have a quiet place to work
- My family and friends are co-operative

Look at the statements you have marked 'S' or 'R'. Write an action plan to improve your study skills in these areas, with a date for you to review how effective you have been.

Writing assignments

- I read through the assignment brief carefully
- I am selective when I read books, articles, and information on the internet, reading only what is relevant
- When I research, I make notes of the key points and details of the reference
- I plan my assignments, and structure the content
- I take short breaks
- I read over my work when I finish and check that I have met all the criteria for the assignment brief
- I give myself a reward when I have finished
- I never wait until the last minute to do assignments

Look at the statements you have marked 'S' or 'R'. Write an action plan to improve your study skills in these areas, with a date for you to review how effective you have been.

Appendix 13: Questionnaire to Evaluate Learner Support

The following form was designed to evaluate learners' perception of the support they receive on a programme from pre-entry to exit.

Learners' Evaluation of Support during the Programme
Pre-programme Choosing your programme: how adequate was the information and guidance you received?
Initial assessment 1. Did you have the opportunity to discuss your long- and short- term goals? *Comment:* 2. If you needed support with any of the following, how satisfied were you with the information and/or arrangements made? Childcare Financial support Transport Literacy/numeracy Disability Learning disability
Induction 1. Did you get as much information as you needed about the content of each session and the assessments? *Comment:* 2. What was done to help you get to know the other learners in the group? *Comment:* 3. How satisfied were you with the study skills guidance you received? *Comment:*

Learning and assessment

1. To what extent were you learning through your preferred learning style?
Comment:

2. How satisfied were you with the frequency and quality of the feedback on your progress?
Comment:

3. How approachable and accessible was your teacher when you needed help?
Comment:

4. How quickly was your work assessed?
Comment:

Progression to further learning or employment

How satisfied were you with the information and guidance given?
Comment:

Appendix 14   The Hairy Toe

The following is a traditional American poem that is a very good exercise for developing tone, pace, volume, pitch, and pause. It can be a solo or a group exercise. Adding movement helps speaking with even more expression.

Once there was a woman went out to pick beans,
And she found a Hairy Toe.
She took the Hairy Toe home with her,
And that night, when she went to bed,
The wind began to moan and groan.
Away off in the distance
She seemed to hear a voice crying,
'Who's got my Hairy Toe?
Who's got my Hair-r-ry To-o-oe?'

The woman scrooched down,
Way down under the covers,
And about that time
The wind appeared to hit the house,
Smoosh,
And the house creaked and cracked
Like something was trying to get in.
The voice had come nearer,
Almost at the door now,
And it said,
'Where's my Hair-r-ry To-o-oe?
Where's my Hair-r-ry To-o-oe?'

The woman scrooched further down
Under the covers
And pulled them tight around her head.
The wind growled around the house
Like some big animal
And r-r-rum-bled
Over the chimbley.
All at once she heard the door cr-r-e-ack
And something slipped in
And began to creep over the floor.
The floor went

Cr-e-eak, cr-e-eak
At every step that thing took towards her bed.
Then in an awful voice it said:
'Where's my Hair-r-ry To-o-oe?
Who's got my Hair-r-ry To-o-oe?
YOU'VE GOT IT!'

Appendix 15:   Religions

The following is an overview of the main world religions, which form just a fraction of all religions and beliefs. Religions can be broadly grouped into:

- Abrahamic
- Indian
- Far Eastern

Abrahamic includes:

- Christianity, which includes Catholics, Protestants, Greek Orthodox, Russian Orthodox, and Oriental Orthodox
- Islam, which includes Sunni, Shi'a, and Sufism
- Judaism, which includes Hasadic and Orthodox
- Baha'i Faith

Indian includes:

- Hinduism
- Buddhism
- Jainism

Far Eastern includes:

- Confucianism
- Taoism
- Shinto

Judaism

Judaism originated around 2000 B.C. when Abraham made a divine covenant with the god of the Israelites. Moses received the Torah, the holy book, from God. Jews believe in one god, and that they are the chosen people and that the Messiah will come some time and there will be a resurrection of the dead. They follow the Ten Commandments.

Orthodox Jews are strict in observing Jewish law. They eat only Kosher food, will not eat milk and meat together, and only eat meat from animals that chew the cud and have a cloven hoof or poultry. Meat has to be killed according to Kosher ritual. Orthodox Jews wear a fringed shawl and small cap when praying. Friday evening to Saturday evening is their holy day. The main religious festivals are:

- The Passover: an eight-day festival commemorating the Exodus from slavery in Egypt, starting with the Seder meal, where unleaven bread is eaten and the story of the deliverance is recounted.
- Rosh Hashana – New Year's Day: ten days of repentance and self-examination.
- Yom Kippur – the Day of Atonement: on the last day of Rosh Hashana, Jews fast for 25 hours, spending the time praying for forgiveness for past sins.

Christianity

Christianity originated as a breakaway sect of Judaism around 2000 years ago. Christians believe that Jesus Christ is the Son of God, born of a virgin, died on a cross to save humans from their sins, and rose again after three days. They believe in original sin and that those who repent of their sins will go to heaven, and those that do not will go to hell.

There have been many breakaway forms of Christianity, but all believe in the concept of one God, who reveals himself as the Trinity: Father, Son, and Holy Spirit. Baptism, which marks the entry of a person into the family of Christ, is the most essential ceremony, while Holy Communion, or the Eucharist, is the principal ceremony where bread and wine are taken, symbolizing the body and blood of Christ. The most important festival is Holy Week, when Christians recall the final week of the life of Jesus: Maundy Thursday, when the Last Supper is commemorated; Good Friday, commemorating the crucifixion of Jesus; Easter Day, when the resurrection is celebrated.

Islam

Muhammad the Prophet founded Islam in Mecca in A.D. 622. Muslims acknowledge the prophets of Judaism and also Jesus Christ, but they do not recognize him as a divine being. Allah, the 'One True God', gave Muhammed the Qur'an, the holy book, which Muslims believe is a clarification of the faith. They believe in hell, where all sinners and unbelievers will go. Muslims who repent will go to Paradise.

Muslims have a duty to observe the Five Pillars of Islam:

- Salat: praying five times a day facing towards Mecca. Face, mouth, ears, forehead, feet, hands, and arms up to the elbow must be washed in running water before praying
- Zajak: giving to charity
- Sawm: fasting during the month of Ramadan
- Hajj: making a pilgrimage to Mecca at least once in one's lifetime
- Shahadah: declaration of faith

The Islamic legal system, Sharia, is based upon the Qur'an and also the sayings of Muhammed. There is no division between the secular and the religious. Religious leaders are called Imams.

Alcohol, gambling, and drugs are forbidden. Muslims do not eat pork or pork products. All other meat must be halal (permissible or lawful), which means slaughtered in a ritual way. Women are expected to dress modestly. The headscarf or hijab is worn by some Muslim women, although not in all Islamic countries. Muslims must be buried (cremation is not permitted) within 24 hours of death. Festivals include Eed-ul-Fitr at the end of Ramadan and Eeed-ul-Azha.

Baha'i Faith

The Baha'i Faith is a breakaway religion of Islam, formed from the teachings of Baha'u'llah in 1844 in Iran. There are no clergy, but there are assembly leaders. They believe that nine great prophets were sent by God to form the main religions. The differences in the religions are due to the needs of the different societies the prophets were addressing. They believe that we all have an immortal soul that is freed after death to travel through the spirit world. They also believe that eventually there will be a world government led by the Baha'is. The faith condemns prejudice and racial disharmony.

Members of this faith fast from sunrise to sunset every year from 2 to 20 March, to mark the end of the old year and to prepare spiritually for the New Year on 21 March. Alcohol is forbidden.

Hinduism

Hinduism is over 4000 years old. It is made up of different religious beliefs, originating in India. Brahman is the universal soul or God, who is worshipped in various forms such as Krishna, Rama, Vishnu or Shiva.

Hindus believe in reincarnation, their soul starting life again in a new body, not necessarily a human one. Depending on how someone has behaved in a previous life, generating good or bad karma, they will be born into a better or worse life. The purpose of life is to realize that we are part of God. This will only happen when we have gone through samsara (cycles of birth, life, and death), accumulating good karma and eventually leaving this plane of existence and rejoining with God.

Hindus have a caste system, believing the caste one is born into is a result of their karma from a previous life. Only Brahmins, the highest caste, can perform religious rituals. Hindus worship in temples, village shrines or at home where they have a shrine to a particular god. There are several scriptures, including the Ramayana (epic poems about Sita and Rama), the Bhagavad Gita, and the Vedas, which are hymns praising the Vedic gods. Key festivals include:

- Diwali: a festival of light

- Holi: a spring festival where bonfires are lit and coloured powder and dyes are thrown over people

Hindus are encouraged to be vegetarians out of respect for all living creatures. There are no dress rules for women but many wear the sari or shalwar-kameez. Married women wear the bindi, a red spot on the forehead.

Buddhism

Buddha is not worshipped as a god. The Buddha was a prince who lived in the fifth century B.C. who went in search of enlightenment, which he found while meditating under a Bodhi tree. He discovered that people could escape the cycle of birth and rebirth and reach Nirvana by following the Four Noble Truths:

- The truth of suffering
- The truth of the origin of suffering
- The truth of the cessation of suffering
- The truth of the path which leads to the cessation of suffering

Buddhists believe that through meditation one can understand the cause of suffering and can free the mind from desire, thereby ceasing to suffer.
  Buddhists live by the Five Moral Principles, which involve refraining from:

- harming living things
- stealing
- sexual misconduct
- lying or gossiping
- taking drugs or drink

The biggest Buddhist festival is Wesak, on 2 June, which celebrates the enlightenment of Buddha. Houses are decorated with lanterns and garlands and some countries release captive birds. Young males often go to live in a temple for a short time to learn about meditation and the philosophy of Buddhism.

Jainism

Jainism has many similarities to Hinduism and Buddhism. Followers believe in reincarnation and karma, but they believe asceticism is the path to enlightenment and liberation from the cycle of birth and rebirth. They only eat food that will not kill the animal or plant from which it is taken. Followers take vows of:

- Ahimsa: non-violence
- Satya: truthfulness
- Asteya: not stealing

- Aparigraha: non-acquisition
- Brahmacarya: chaste living

Confucianism

Confucianism has developed from the teachings of Confucius, who lived from 551 B.C. to 479 B.C. Confucius's goal was social harmony, with well-ordered families, a well-ordered state, and a well-ordered world. He taught that this would be achieved through striving to be a perfect man, which involved much ritual, filial piety, and duty.

The rituals help people to know their place in society and to whom they should display piety: the subject to the sovereign, child to parent, wife to husband, younger person to older person. This has led to ancestor worship. Confucius also taught that when rulers behaved in a moral way towards their subjects, their subjects would behave morally towards their children, and children would behave morally. Confucius believed that if a person felt a duty not to do wrong or make mistakes, then there would be shame or 'losing face' if they transgressed, and therefore they would be less likely to do so.

One of the many sayings of Confucius is that what you do not want done to yourself, do not do to others. He encouraged people to be polite and considerate towards others, and not to act out of self-interest or for personal gain. Benevolence towards others is the highest Confucian virtue.

Taoism

Tao means 'the path' or 'the way'. Taoism is to do with pursuing the path of harmony internally and externally. It arose from the teachings of Lao-Tse, who was a contemporary of Confucius, with a philosophy that did not focus on rituals and duties.

Taoists strive for balance in the body, believing illness is caused by blockages caused by a lack of balance in the body's chi (internal energy). They practise Tai Chi, a form of exercise that works on all parts of the body. There is great emphasis on the harmony of opposites: yin, the dark side, and yang, the light side. The Three Jewels to guide one's life are:

- Compassion
- Moderation
- Humility

Diet is frugal, consisting mainly of cereal, but every ten to fifteen days there is a festival, each one associated with particular foods. For example, the Dragon Boat festival is associated with steamed dumplings and rice in bamboo leaves, while the mid-autumn festival is associated with moon cakes.

Shinto

Shinto, which originated in Japan around 500 B.C., means 'the way of the gods'. It is an animistic belief system, revering nature. Followers worship kami (spirits), who inhabit our world and make mistakes like humans. The most important kami is Amaterasu, the sun goddess, who is an ancestress of the Imperial Family. Another kami is Mount Fuji. A spirit can be in an animate or inanimate object or even a concept. This love of nature extends into the Japanese interest in flower arranging and garden design.

There are Four Affiliations:

- Tradition and the family, where family preserves tradition
- Love of nature: as nature is sacred, natural objects are worshipped
- Physical cleanliness
- Matsun – festivals that honour the spirits

The religion gives guidance on rituals and methods that foster relations between humans and with the spirits. Unlike other religions, it does not focus on how to prepare for life after death.

When a family member dies, and they find peace, they become revered ancestors who protect the family. Every summer they are welcomed home during the Obon festival. If, however, they are not at peace when they die, they become yurei (tormented ghosts) who can cause trouble and therefore have to be appeased. Purification rituals are very common, using water or salt. Purification rituals take place when a new house is built or a new car or aeroplane. People often sprinkle salt around their house or put a dish of salt at the front door for good luck.

Shrines may be guarded by pairs of lion-dogs who ward off evil spirits. In January at the Fire Festival, shrine decorations are burnt to bring good health and a good harvest. Sumo wrestling was originally a Shinto ritual to bring about a good harvest.

Bibliography

Aldridge, F. and Tuckett, A. (2007) *What Older People Learn*. Leicester: NIACE.

Anderson, L.W., Krathwohl, D.R., Airasian, P.W., Cruickshank, K.A., Mayer, R.E., Pintrich P.R. *et al.* (eds) (2001) *A Taxonomy for Learning, Teaching and Assessment: A Revision of Bloom's Taxonomy of Educational Objectives*. New York: Addison Wesley Longman.

Berne, E. (1996) *Games People Play*. New York: Random House.

Braun, E.M. and Davis, R.D. (1997) *The Gift of Dyslexia: Why Some of the Brightest People Can't Read and How They Can Learn*, 2nd revised edn. London: Souvenir Press.

Clarke, A. (2006) *Teaching Adults ITC Skills*. Exeter: Learning Matters.

Clarke, A. and Hesse, C. (2006) *Online Resources in the Classroom*. Leicester: NIACE.

Cottrell, S. (2003) *The Study Skills Handbook*, 2nd edn. Basingstoke: Palgrave Study Guides.

Curzon, L.B. (2003) *Teaching in Further Education*. London: Continuum International Publishing Group.

Ellis, A. (2005) *How to Stubbornly Refuse to Make Yourself Miserable about Anything – Yes, Anything!*, revised edn. Sacramento, CA: Citadel Press.

Gardner, H. (2006) *Multiple Intelligences – New Horizons in Theory and Practice*, 2nd revised edn. New York: Basic Books.

Gravells, A. (2007) *Preparing to Teach in the Lifelong Learning Sector*. Exeter: Learning Matters.

Hardcastle, P. (2004) *Digital Cameras in Teaching and Learning*. Leicester: NIACE.

Harris, T.A. (1995) *I'm OK – You're OK*. London: Arrow Books.

Honey, P. and Mumford, A. (2006) *Learning Styles Questionnaire: 80 Items Version*, revised edn. Maidenhead: Peter Honey Publications.

Knowles, M.S., Holton, E.F. and Swanson, R.A. (2005) *The Adult Learner: The Definitive Classic in Adult Education and Human Resource Development*, 6th edn. Oxford: Butterworth-Heinemann.

Kolb, D.A. (1984) *Experiential Learning: Experience as the Source of Learning and Development*. London: Financial Times/Prentice-Hall.

Lazear, D. (2004) *Higher Order Thinking: The Multiple Intelligences Way*. Brookline, MA: Zephyr Press.

Maslow, A.H. (1998) *Towards a Psychology of Being*, 3rd edn. New York: John Wiley.

McLeod, J. (2007) *Counselling Skills*. Maidenhead: McGraw-Hill.

Mearns, D. and Thorne, B. (2007) *Person-Centred Counselling in Action*. London: Sage Publications.

Mehrabian, A. (2007) *Nonverbal Communication*. Piscataway, NJ: Aldine Transaction.

Moon, J. (2006) *Learning Journals*. London: Routledge.

Petty, G. (2004) *Teaching Today*, 3rd edn. Cheltenham: Nelson Thornes.

Reece, I. and Walker, S. (2003) *Teaching, Training and Learning*, 2nd edn. Houghton-le-Spring, UK: Business Education Publishers Ltd.

Ridge, J. (2002) *The Complete Voice and Speech Workout*. New York: Applause Theatre Book Publishers.

Rogers, B. (1997) *You Know the Fair Rule*, 2nd edn. London: Financial Times/Prentice-Hall.

Rogers, B. (2006) *Classroom Behaviour*, 2nd edn. London: Paul Chapman.

Rogers, C.R. (1995) *A Way of Being*. Boston, MA: Houghton Mifflin.

Rogers, J. (2007) *Adults Learning*, 5th edn. Maidenhead: McGraw-Hill.

Rogers, J. (2008) *Coaching Skills*, 2nd edn. Maidenhead: McGraw-Hill.

Sanders, P. (2002) *First Steps in Counselling*. Ross-on-Wye: PCCS Books.

Scales, P. (2008) *Teaching in the Lifelong Learning Sector*. Maidenhead: McGraw-Hill.

Schön, D. (1991) *The Reflective Practitioner*. Aldershot: Ashgate.

Stewart, I. and Joines, V. (1987) *TA Today – A New Introduction to Transactional Analysis*. Melton Mowbray: Lifespace Publishers.

Thompson, J. (2002) *Community Education and Neighbourhood Renewal*. Leicester: NIACE.

Trower, P., Casey, A. and Dryden, W. (1988) *Cognitive-Behavioural Counselling in Action*. London: Sage Publications.

Tuckman, B. (1965) Developmental sequence in small groups, *Psychological Bulletin*, 63, 384–99.

Tummons, J. (2007a) *Becoming a Professional Tutor in the Lifelong Learning Sector*. Exeter: Learning Matters.

Tummons, J. (2007b) *Assessing Learning in the Lifelong Learning Sector*, 2nd edn. Exeter: Learning Matters.

Wallace, S. (2007a) *Getting the Buggers Motivated in FE*. London: Continuum International Group.

Wallace, S. (2007b) *Managing Behaviour in the Lifelong Learning Sector*, 2nd edn. Exeter: Learning Matters.

Wallace, S. (2007c) *Teaching, Tutoring and Training in the Lifelong Learning Sector*. Exeter: Learning Matters.

Useful websites

womensaid.org.uk
www.addaction.org.uk
www.bbc.co.uk/religion
www.bbc.c.uk/science/humanbody/mind
www.aaia.org.uk
www.citizensadvice.org.uk
www.connexions-direct.com
www.dius.gov.uk/publications
www.iamdyslexia.com
www.equality/humanrights.com

www.geoffpetty.com
www.ifl.ac.uk
www.lifelonglearninguk.org
www.nas.org.uk
www.open.ac.uk/inclusiveteaching
www.peterhoney.com
www.qca.org.uk
www.samaritans.org
www.slamnet.org.uk/assessment
www.techdis.ac.uk
www.vark-learn.com

Index

Diagrams are listed in italics